SEAN DORMAN, as a boy of
Irish public school, was awarded
and the English master regularly
Form. He became editor of the
winner of an essay competition
Great Britain and Ireland. After graduating at Oxford, he worked
as a freelance journalist in London, having articles published in
some twenty British and Irish periodicals. He also ghosted half
a dozen non-fiction books for a publisher. He had a burlesque
of Chekhov staged by the Dublin Gate Theatre, a radio play
broadcast by Radio Eireann, and he published a few short stories,
one being broadcast by the BBC. For five and a half years
in Dublin he published a literary, theatre and art magazine,
Commentary. In England, from 1957 until a few years ago, he
ran the Sean Dorman Manuscript Society for mutual criticism, a
Society still run by others under the same name and listed in *The
Writers' and Artists' Year Book*. His magazine *Writing*, also
listed during its career in 'The Year Book', was founded in 1959,
and sold after twenty-six years. While his family was growing
up, he had to seek a more regular income, and taught secondary
school French and junior German for some twenty-six years. To
make up for lost time, between 1983 and 1993 he wrote and
published, under the imprint of his Raffeen Press, eleven books.
They embraced novels, autobiography, essays, a three-act play,
theatre criticism, short-stories and a solitary poem. Many of the
books were re-writes or extensions, now allowed to go out of
print, so the present tally is seven. Five of these have been included
in his three-volume hardback, *The Selected Works of Sean
Dorman*, now gradually finding its way into national and
university libraries throughout the world.

For LENNOX ROBINSON
my late uncle and godfather, playwright,
sometime director of the Abbey Theatre, Dublin;
D. Litt, Dublin University

Also by Sean Dorman

BRIGID AND THE MOUNTAIN
a novel

PORTRAIT OF MY YOUTH
an autobiography

RED ROSES FOR JENNY
a novel

THE MADONNA
a novel

PHYSICIANS, PRIESTS AND PHYSICISTS
essays

SEX AND THE REVEREND STRONG
a novel (printing)

and published by The Raffeen Press

Further copies of
THE STRONG MAN
may be obtained through
WH Smith and other good bookshops.
Also from The Raffeen Press
Union Place, Fowey, Cornwall PL23 1BY.

THE STRONG MAN

Sean Dorman

THE RAFFEEN PRESS

Cover illustration: MADELEINE DORMAN

THE STRONG MAN
A RAFFEEN PRESS BOOK 1 901243 05 2

PRINTING HISTORY
In paperback: *The Strong Man* 1989
Raffeen Press reissued in paperback 1997

Copyright © Sean Dorman 1997

All rights reserved. No part of this publication may be reproduced,
stored in a retrieval system or transmitted, in any form or by
any means electronic, mechanical, photocopying, recording
or otherwise, without prior permission of the copyright owner.

Conditions of Sale
This book is sold subject to the condition that it shall not,
by way of trade, or otherwise, be lent, re-sold, hired out or otherwise
circulated without the publisher's prior consent in any form of binding
or cover other than that in which it is published and without a
similar condition including this condition being imposed on the
subsequent purchaser.

Printed and bound in Great Britain by Short Run Press Ltd, Exeter.

The Strong Man
Sean Dorman

The Strong Man, a comedy in three acts, can lay no claims either to distinction or to having been performed on a stage. But it can claim to have been read by a considerable number of people who have reported that it caused them not only to smile but, on occasion, to laugh outright. Should something that has given rise to smiles, and even laughter, be left upon a shelf, or be entombed in a drawer? Of course not. It should be produced in a book. Also produced in this book are three theatre critiques. In days gone by, Ireland gave to literature great playwrights from that seeming hotbed of dramatic genius, Dublin University: William Congreve, George Farquhar, Oliver Goldsmith. Since then there have been: John Millington Synge, Samuel Beckett (both from the same university), William Butler Yeats, Oscar Wilde, Bernard Shaw, Sean O'Casey. Well known, but perhaps less well known than they ought to be, are Denis Johnston and Teresa Deevy. I have devoted a critique to each of them. Also to William Shakespeare, an Englishman, I'm told. The trouble with William Shakespeare, is that he has been allowed, unfortunately, to develop into a cult figure. Not only are his great plays produced, but his lesser pieces also are reverently laid out upon the stage, thus almost certainly denying many hours of theatre time to others with better work to offer. Such a lesser piece, here reviewed, is *Twelve Night*.

THE STRONG MAN

An Absurdity in Three Acts

ACT ONE

Characters in order of their appearance in the play: Mrs Quin; Peggy Quin, her daughter; Colonel Sir Henry Robinson, their landlord; Chris, Peggy's fiance; Eamonn, an artist; Mr Murphy, a business man; Norah, daughter of Mrs Quin's gardener; Father McMahon, the parish priest; Dr O'Donovan, the family doctor.

(The curtain rises on a stately room belonging to a prosperous Irish country house. There is a door on the right, up stage, leading to the hall and the front door. Up stage, centre, a French window gives into the garden. A summer sun is shining. Between the door and the French window, a telephone hangs on the wall. In the centre of the left-hand wall is a door, at the moment open, leading into another room, unseen. A mirror hangs on this wall.

The centre of the stage is taken up with a table loaded with silver toast-racks, sets of china, electric kettles, glass wear. They look remarkably like wedding presents. There is a smaller table, left, with some bric-a-brac on it, including an Indian ornament.

A middle-aged lady, Mrs Quin, stands behind the bigger table. She has a pleasantly eager face, having managed to preserve her capacity for a girlish excitement about life through the horrors of marriage and the relief of widowhood. At the moment, she is rearranging the presents. She picks up a parcel and looks it over with a puzzled expression. She glances towards the other room and calls.)

Mrs Quin: Peggy! (*No answer. Louder*) Peggy!
Peggy: (*off*) Yes, Mother?
She enters. She is twenty-three, pretty, attractively dressed, and possesses an air of competence and determination.

Mrs Quin: Did you leave this packet on the table, dear?

Peggy: No, Mother. (*She has crossed to Mrs Quin and put her arm affectionately round her waist. She looks at the parcel.*) I suppose it must be one of the wedding presents, Mumsie.

Mrs Quin: There's no name or anything. (*She opens it, and discovers a silver toast-rack.*) Oh, a toast-rack! Just fancy! (*She holds out a label attached to it and reads.*) 'To Peggy, on her wedding day, from the Colonel.' Well, isn't that original of the Colonel!

Peggy: (*picking up a toast-rack in each hand from the dozen or so on the table and looking at them*) It was sweet of him.

Mrs Quin: And he's written some poetry. (*Reads*) 'To be successful as a host

This is the secret you need to learn most,

Better than dumpling and better than roast

Is a jolly bit of British well-crisped toast.'

Well, isn't that very good? Such — such verve. (*She sighs.*) 'To Peggy, on her wedding day . . .'

Peggy: (*replacing the toast-racks*) Why the sigh, Mumsie darling?

Mrs Quin: It set me thinking of the last wedding anniversary Dad and I celebrated before he died. (*She kisses her daughter on the cheek.*) And now our only little daughter has grown up all in a few years and is going to be married.

Peggy: (*laughing*) You know you adore Chris and have hardly been able to wait to marry me off to him.

Mrs Quin: I know. But when the actual moment has come . . . (*She puts the Colonel's toast-rack with the rest.*) Just like the Colonel, to give you a present. By the way, where is Sir Henry?

Peggy: Where d'you suppose! Out in the garden clipping the hedge.

Mrs Quin: I wish all landlords made a hobby of clipping their tenants' hedges.

Peggy: (*imitating Sir Henry*) Not landlord. (*She twirls an imaginary moustache.*) Friend of the family.

Mrs Quin: And a real good friend. Well, when the gardener gets this new under-gardener of his, there won't be many hedge-clipping opportunities left for Sir Henry.

Peggy: Is Murphy getting someone to help him in the garden?

Mrs Quin: Trust Murphy for that!

Peggy: Yes. It's about the only thing on which he'd bestir himself — getting someone else to do his work.

Mrs Quin: You're so right. Now, what was I saying?

Peggy: It was about Murphy and the new under-gardener.

Mrs Quin: Before that. Oh yes, when the actual moment has come to give you away. But then, you and Chris were so obviously made for one another.

Peggy: I wonder if we were.

Mrs Quin: (*rather sharply*) What's that?

Peggy: Mother — Mother, do you think it is good for — for people who have been very close together — almost brother and sister, in fact — do you think it's good for them to marry?

Mrs Quin: How do you mean, dear?

Peggy: Well, Chris and me. Playing tennis against one another from almost the moment we could hold a racquet. It's — it's almost like inter-marriage.

Mrs Quin: (*very disturbed*) Chris is a fine boy. A — a fine boy.

Peggy: I think you think of him as your own son, Mother.

Mrs Quin: Sure, you were only joking?

Peggy: (*hugging her*) I was only joking.

(*An elderly military-looking man sweeps in through the french windows, his big bright teeth, which he bares incessantly like a good-natured tiger, smiling under his grey moustache. His large fierce grey eyebrows threaten one good-humouredly. He is wearing khaki shirt and shorts. He holds one hand to his chest as though he had hurt it.*)

Sir Henry: Ah, there you are, Mrs Quin! Looking at the presents as usual!

Mrs Quin: Looking at *your* present, Sir Henry.

(*She picks up the wrong toast-rack and dangles it before him.*)

Peggy: (*hastily taking it from her and handing her another*) This one, Mother.

Mrs Quin: Ah, yes, how could I have made such a silly mistake!

Sir Henry: See you've one or two other toast-racks.

Peggy: Ah, but not one with — with such wide spaces for the toast.

Mrs Quin: So many toast-racks these days have got such *narrow* spaces.

Sir Henry: (*pleased*) Really? You don't say!

Mrs Quin: And then, the poetry. It reminded me of — of Tennyson.

Sir Henry: Did it in half an hour while resting after tiffin. (*Murmurs appreciatively*) 'A jolly bit of British well-crisped toast.'

Mrs Quin: Colonel, you keep holding your hand as though you had hurt it.

Sir Henry: Nothing. Nothing. Little tumble from the ladder while I was clipping the hedge.

Mrs Quin: (*having looked at the hand more closely*) It's a really bad cut.

Sir Henry: Not quite that. Came in to see if you had a bandage or something.

Mrs Quin: Oh, good gracious me! (*She gives a piercing shriek towards the hall.*) Evie! Evie! (*To the Colonel*) You unfortunate man! You'll bleed to death. Murphy should never have given you the clippers. He can look for other work. I'll not keep him another day.

Sir Henry: Wasn't your gardener's fault. I insisted —

Mrs Quin: Well, thank heavens he's getting an assistant. That'll stop all this ghastly bloodshed. Evie! Evie! Where is that girl? She's never to be found when she's wanted. Peggy, run and telephone Dr O'Donovan. And get the bottle of iodine from my bedroom. Tell Evie to bring up some hot water. Evie! Evie!

(*Ignoring her mother's directions, Peggy has, with complete self-possession, taken charge of the situation. She examines the wound.*)

Peggy: Mother, bring some hot water. Put a little Jeyes Fluid into it.

Mrs Quin: Oh dear. Jeyes Fluid. Hot water. Evie! Drat that girl!

Peggy: I thought I saw her coming out of the pantry about half an hour ago.

Mrs Quin: I'll have to do it myself. Jeyes Fluid. Hot water. Hot water. Jeyes Fluid . . . (*Her voice trails away into the distance as she fusses out of the room by the door, left, leading to the other room.*)

Sir Henry: Ought to be a nurse, young lady.

Peggy: D'you think so, Colonel?

Sir Henry: Different as chalk from cheese, you and your ma. She goes all to pieces. No steadiness under fire.

Peggy: Poor Mother. She hates an emergency.

Sir Henry: And you love it.

Peggy: Sir Henry!

Sir Henry: Taking charge and looking after people — that's you.

Peggy: I certainly sometimes feel my life to be — oh, I don't know — useless. It's too easy.

Sir Henry: (*nodding decisively*) The whole trouble between Chris and you.

Peggy: (*after a pause*) So you've noticed?

Sir Henry: He doesn't need looking after. Is there another man?

Peggy: Good heavens, Colonel, no. Mother seems to have seen to that.

Sir Henry: Worse and worse, my dear. If you feel this way when there isn't another man, how are you going to feel when the other man comes along?

Peggy: The other man?

Sir Henry: (*nodding, and pointing, right, to the door leading into the hall*) Might walk in through that door at this moment. Chris here soon?

Peggy: Any minute.

Sir Henry: Talk it over.

Peggy: (*after a pause*) All right. Hush! Mother.

(*Mrs Quin hurricanes into the room cargoed with a mountain of curative impedimenta, including a kettle of hot water, a basin, bottle of disinfectant, towels, etc.*)

Mrs Quin: How are you, Sir Henry? (*To Peggy*) How is he?

Peggy: Did you find Evie?

Mrs Quin: I thought I saw her moving in the garden. But it was only Chancie chasing a rat.

(*The front door bell, right, is heard.*)

Peggy: I suppose Evie *will* answer the door.

Mrs Quin: Oh I hope so. I do hope so.

Peggy: That must be our pet Strong Man.

Mrs Quin: How can you talk about Chris like that in front of the Colonel!

Peggy: (*washing Sir Henry's hand*) I'm sorry, Mother. But I sometimes wish he wouldn't talk physical culture twenty-four hours a day. I bet his first words will be: what, over-dressed on a beautiful day like this! Expose the skin to the ultra-violet.

(*Chris strides briskly into the room, chest out and shoulders back. He is large, athletic and twenty-five. He is wearing tennis shorts and singlet, and is sunburnt to a chocolate colour.*)

Chris: I rang long and loud. Where's Evie? I had to let myself in. (*He kisses Peggy perfunctorily.*) Hurt your hand, Colonel?

Mrs Quin: Thanks to Murphy. I'll be relieved when the new under-gardener comes to —

Chris: (*interrupting, and gazing round at them*) Good heavens, just look at you all! Over-dressed on a beautiful day like this! Look at me. Expose the skin to the ultra-violet.

(*Peggy casts her eyes to heaven.*)

Mrs Quin: I was sitting by the window all the morning, enjoying the sun.

Chris: (*sharply*) Was the window closed?

Mrs Quin: Why — why yes, I think so.

Chris: (*very earnestly*) No use, Mrs Quin. The ultra-violet can't penetrate through ordinary glass. I advise you most earnestly to open it in future.

Peggy: There he goes!

Chris: We need all the ultra-violet we can get, within reason. It activates the ergesterol under the skin and forms vitamin D, necessary for the teeth and bones. (*He lowers his voice confidentially.*) Did you have rickets when you were young? Are your teeth getting loose?

Mrs Quin: (*starting back*) Good gracious! I hope not.

Chris: (*cheerily, walking over to the French windows*) Never mind. There's nothing that a three weeks' fast won't cure. Nature Cure has taught us that. (*During the ensuing conversation, he takes a step out into the sunshine and does a few bending exercises.*)

Mrs Quin: Those Nature Cure people you're always talking about — Dr Hurst up in Dublin told me they were quacks.

Chris: Professional jealousy. They cure; Dr Hurst kills. The quack is Dr Hurst.

Mrs Quin: (*in dignified reproof*) Dr Hurst is a specialist.

Chris: The very quintessance of quackery, since all disease is interconnected. Fitzwilliam Square is filled with quacks.

Mrs Quin: Dear, dear. I don't know how any of us keep alive.

Chris: By keeping out of Fitzwilliam Square.

Peggy: You can't deny that doctors know a lot about disease.

Chris: And almost nothing about health. They swallow the same alcoholic poisons as their patients, smoke the same nicotine and tar, eat the same debased and ill-balanced diets, live the same sedentary lives, and are consequently crippled by the same diseases. They cannot speach health, because they do not practice it.

Mrs Quin: After all, what is health?

Chris: Its a way of life.

Peggy: One that we haven't all got time to live.

Chris: If you haven't got time to be well, it's certain that, sooner or later, you'll have to take off time to be ill. So you lose the happiness that health brings, and get no more work done.

Peggy: But show some moderation. People think you're a crank.

Chris: One must stick to one's guns. Never give way to the pressure of opinion; only to the pressure of truth.

Peggy: (*completing the bandaging*) There you are, Colonel.

Sir Henry: Thank you, m'dear.

(*She defiantly takes out a cigarette from a cigarette-box on the table and lights it.*)

Chris: (*advancing fiercely towards her*) Where did you get those cigarettes?

Peggy: A wedding present.

Chris: After we're married, there'll be no smoking for you.

Peggy: Then we won't get married.

Chris: We'll see about that!

Peggy: (*seizing a chest-expander off the table and dangling it before his eyes*) There's my present to you. I suppose you're giving me a raw vegetable shredder?

Chris: And a very good present it would be if I did.

Mrs Quin: Come, Colonel, they're quarrelling again. Let's go out into the garden.

(*Sir Henry bows his acquiescence and they move towards the French windows.*)

Mrs Quin: When they're quarrelling, they aren't fit company for anyone.

(*They go out, leaving the two young people feeling a little foolish.*)

Peggy: Mother's quite right. Chris — Chris, we don't really suit one another. You don't need me. I want to help someone. Perhaps I ought to be a nurse.

Chris: I suppose you'd like me to go out into the garden and cut my hand off!

Peggy: N-o-o. But if it could happen, just now and again, by accident.

Chris: It could happen only twice. Look! Only two hands. (*He regards her suspiciously.*) Peggy, what's the exact point you are making?

Peggy: The hopelessness of our getting married.

Chris: What are you talking about? We're going to be married in a week —

Peggy: I know, but —

Chris: — Father McMahon is coming here this afternoon to make final arrangements —

Peggy: I've had that on my mind, only —

Chris: — the table is groaning under toast-racks and coffee sets —

Peggy: I've thought of that, yet —

Chris: — your mother has the house in an uproar and is careering towards the port of matrimony with all sails set —

Peggy: That's the worst of all —

Chris: — and you talk about the hopelessness of our getting married!

Peggy: But in your heart of hearts you agree with me.

Chris: I do not. We've everything in common. We — we both come of good families, we're both Catholics, we're both frantically fond of tennis —

Peggy: Tennis! That's just about the measure of the usefulness of our lives.

Chris: Let's not quarrel. Listen, I've a surprise for you.

Peggy: A new system of exercises?

Chris: I haven't quite the one-track mind you imagine. My present to you — you'll never guess what it is in a hundred years.

Peggy: (*turning her back*) You can keep your present to yourself. I don't want to know what it is. I'm not interested. What is it?
Chris: I've arranged to have your portrait painted.
Peggy: (*swinging round delightedly*) My portrait! (*She recollects herself, and turns back again. She speaks in a casual tone.*) My portrait? Really. Who by?
Chris: Ah, wouldn't you like to know!
Peggy: (*all impatience*) Who by?
Chris: Ah.

(*She goes to him, and he backs away. She catches his arm and shakes him.*)

Peggy: Who by, who by, who by?
Chris: By an artist, of course.
Peggy: (*sighing it out*) An artist. (*Pause.*) How did you arrange it? When does he come?
Chris: Through a big businessman.

(*She runs over to the French windows and calls.*)

Peggy: Mother! Mother! Sir Henry!
Mrs Quin: (*from the garden*) Yes, dear?
Peggy: Come in! Come in quickly! (*She returns from the windows.*) Do Mother and the Colonel know about this?

(*He nods. She looks at him with a new admiration.*)

Peggy: Aren't you a dark horse! (*She feels his biceps, and he purrs.*) What's the artist's name?
Chris: Oh, some big Dublin artist. I left all that to the businessman. He'll be here today to make arrangements.
Peggy: A big Dublin artist! He'll be tall, distinguished, have a long black car, and a beard. He'll be about forty-seven and a quarter years of age. I love men about forty-seven and a quarter years of age.
Chris: (*jealous*) I think twenty-five is a much better age. Men of forty-seven are so — so forty-sevenish.

(*Mrs Quin and Sir Henry enter.*)

Peggy: My portrait!
(*They both laugh.*)
Peggy: I always knew that more went on inside that clever head of

his than dumb-bells and chest-expanders. We shall all have to listen to him with respect now on the subject of art.

Chris: (*drawing himself up in a pontifical tone*) There's a great deal of nonsense spoken on the subject of art. Art is, after all, art.

Mrs Quin: (*in admiration*) Art is art. How true!

Chris: Much of what passes for art nowadays is not art. What is art?

Mrs Quin: (*gazing into his eyes*) Yes, dear?

Chris: Er — art is — er — that which has been created by the artist.

Mrs Quin: (*nodding eagerly*) — created by the artist. Yes. Yes, I see that. (*To the others*) He throws such a fresh light on it!

Peggy: (*taking Sir Henry's arm*) Colonel, what do you think of art and artists?

Sir Henry: Art? Highest respect for it. There were several of those artist chaps with my regiment in 1942. Did a fine job — painting camouflage.

Peggy: But I mean, really important painting?

Sir Henry: What could be more important than camouflage? I remember once when it saved a whole battery —

Mrs Quin: Don't you think Frazer Henryson is one of the finest of living English artists?

Sir Henry: That fellah! He's no good. He was a conschie in 1939.

Mrs Quin: But I read that he was a splendid draughtsman.

Sir Henry: Splendid draughtsman? A conscientious objector?

Peggy: (*to herself*) Tall, distinguished, forty-seven and a quarter . . .

(*Sir Henry chucks Peggy under the chin, but addresses himself to Chris.*)

Sir Henry: My boy, I'd look out for myself! These bright eyes at the mention of an artist!

(*Chris looks annoyed. He glances at his watch and crosses to the French windows. He stares out.*)

Mrs Quin: Are you expecting anyone, Chris?

Chris: Eh? Er — no, no. (*He returns into the room.*)

Sir Henry: (*to Mrs Quin*) Come and look at my hedge.

Mrs Quin: Certainly, Sir Henry. But no more clipping.

Sir Henry: (*mournfully*) No more clipping?

(*They move towards the French windows.*)

Mrs Quin: I shall put the clippers under lock and key until the new under-gardener arrives.

Sir Henry: (*looking back at Peggy*) You've a heartless mother. Will you look at my hedge?

Peggy: Of course, Sir Henry.

Sir Henry: (*to Chris*) You?

(*Chris glances at his watch again, and then towards the windows.*)

Chris: Another time, Colonel.

Peggy: He *is* expecting someone. The artist?

Chris: Why are you so eager to meet him?

Peggy: Just — interested.

(*She and the others go out.*)

Chris: Four thirty. They should be here if they caught the train. (*He returns to the French windows.*) There they are! (*He goes out, right, into the hall. Almost at once his voice is heard.*) Hello, Murphy! Come in. This way, Murphy. And your friend. (*He re-enters.*) So you followed my directions successfully. Found your way up from the station.

(*Mr Murphy is a brisk man. He glances briskly about the room as though he hoped to snap up the opportunity to do a brisk piece of business. He has a sharp, lively, ingenious face. His suit, linen and shoes are smart and flashy, but his side pockets bulge. He is middle-aged, and speaks with a Northern Ireland accent. He is followed by a young man, slightly built, whose shabby clothes, and eyes ever on the look-out for a chance to scrounge, bespeak the artist of distinction. Notwithstanding the pallor of poverty, he is distinctly handsome.*)

Murphy: Only just caught the train. Had a big business deal to complete. By the way, I rang twice. No one came. Perhaps your front door bell is out of order. If so, the Murphy electric Melody Man is just what you need. When the button is pressed, it plays *Mother MacCree* over and over again until the door is opened.

Chris: Damn that girl Evie!

Murphy: Allow me to introduce Eamonn O'Sullivan.

(*Chris looks at Eamonn O'Sullivan's appearance somewhat askance.*)

Chris: Pleased to meet you.

Eamonn: (*in a Cockney accent*) 'ullo, mate!

Chris: Eamonn O'Sullivan! Sounds Irish of the Irish! It's you that are painting my fiancee's portrait, isn't it?

Eamonn: Got it in one, mate.

Chris: Mr O'Sullivan, you have an English accent. Your name led me to suppose —

Eamonn: Quite so. I'm an Englishman who has spent six weeks in Ireland, that is, I'm a convinced nationalist and dye-in-the-wool Irish language revivalist. My name is really Perkins — Bert Perkins.

Chris: (*laughing*) Bert Perkins!

Eamonn: There being no suitable Irish translation, I was obliged to adopt a nom-de-plume, as you might say.

Murphy: Dia's muire agath.

Eamonn: (*startled*) Eh? Oh, Irish! I've only got as far as: Ta me. Where did you learn to speak Irish, Murphy? Why is it that Presbyterians from the North, when they come South, are always more nationalist than the Catholic southerners themselves? (*To Chris*) Mr Murphy tramped into Dublin twenty years ago without as much as twenty shillings in his pocket, and has proceeded since then to built up the biggest emporium in town without any fuss whatever.

Chris: Indeed!

Murphy: We don't make a fuss in the North. Apart, of course, from the Pope and the Battle of the Boyne. We are driven into hysteria at the mention of that inoffensive churchman or that singularly uninspiring little skirmish.

Chris: Mrs Quin will be back soon. I know she would like me to show you your rooms.

Murphy: We left our bags down at the lodge with her gardener. I'll just walk down —

Chris: I'll come with you. We can talk business on the way. I'll get the gardener — a namesake of yours, Murphy — his name is Murphy too.

Murphy: Murphy, eh!

Chris: I'll get him to bring up your bags on the trolley.

Eamonn: I'll leave you two to talk business.

Chris: Make yourself at home. The others will be in presently.

(*He is just leaving the room, right, Murphy having already preceded him into the hall, when Sir Henry enters through the French windows.*)

Chris: (*calling over his shoulder*) Hello, Colonel. This is the man Murphy was getting. Would you look after him?

(*He goes.*)

Sir Henry: (*to himself*) Man Murphy was getting? Of course. (*He walks up to Eamonn.*) You're the man who's going to work with Murphy in the garden?

Eamonn: (*mystified*) I didn't know we were going to work out of doors.

Sir Henry: Certainly, my man. Where else?

Eamonn: Well, now that I think of it, that's rather a good idea of Murphy's. In this weather, what could be pleasanter.

(*Sir Henry is visibly shaken at this casual attitude on the part of a member of the lower orders.*)

Eamonn: You would be Miss Peggy Quin's grandfather?

Sir Henry: No, sir. Friend of the family.

Eamonn: I hope we become close friends too.

Sir Henry: Indeed!

Eamonn: (*producing cigarettes*) Cigarette?

Sir Henry: (*coldly*) I smoke a pipe.

(*Eamonn coolly lights up under the outraged stare of the Colonel.*)

Eamonn: (*inspecting the room*) I think I'm going to like it here.

Sir Henry: Mrs Quin treats her servants well.

Eamonn: Eh? Oh, her servants.

(*He lowers himself into a chair.*)

Sir Henry: Look here —

Eamonn: (*glancing out through the windows*) A tennis court! Never learnt how to play. I dare say Miss Quin would soon teach me, eh?

Sir Henry: (*to himself*) Socialism!

Eamonn: Excuse me?

Sir Henry: Look here, won't Murphy be expecting you down at the lodge?

Eamonn: Oh no, he'll be back shortly. I hear that Mrs Quin has a positively luxurious bathroom. Murphy and I are looking forward to having a jolly good wallow in it before tea.

(*Sir Henry starts.*)

Eamonn: This Miss Quin — as man to man — is she pretty?

Sir Henry: Look here, sir — Yes, she's very pretty.

Eamonn: Between you and me, I'm very susceptible.

Sir Henry: Young man, evidently something I have to make plain. You're here to work and give satisfaction. If you do, you'll be well treated.

Eamonn: (*astonished*) I'm ready to start at once.

Sir Henry: (*in better humour*) Ah! Give you a word of friendly warning, my man. Garden clippers are sharp. (*He holds up his injured hand in evidence.*)

Eamonn: (*now fully assured of the Colonel's insanity*) Really! I must be very careful.

Sir Henry: Suggest you make a start at once with your work.

Eamonn: Certainly. Where's Miss Quin?

Sir Henry: Again! Thought I'd made it clear you were to attend to your work and not get ideas above your station.

(*Eamonn is now thoroughly alarmed. He rises and puts his chair between himself and the Colonel.*)

Eamonn: How can I work, with or without a clippers, without Miss Quin?

Sir Henry: What's Miss Quin got to do with it?

Eamonn: I need her to pose for me. I need her to inspire me.

Sir Henry: (*muttering*) New kind of Communism!

Eamonn: (*thoughtfully*) I don't suppose she'd consider posing for me in the nude.

Sir Henry: (*muttering*) Free love! Must be a member of the Transport and General Workers' Union. (*To Eamonn*) Sir, as long as you are working here, Miss Quin will never so much as allow you to set eyes on her.

(*Eamonn stares at Sir Henry, than sets himself to humour a doting old man.*)

Eamonn: I quite understand. Yes, yes indeed. Now what would you like me to paint?

Sir Henry: Paint, sir? I don't know of anything that needs any paint. Unless you put a slap of tar on the old pigsty.

(*Peggy enters, left, by the inner door.*)

Peggy: I thought I heard you talking to someone, Sir Henry.

Sir Henry: Ah, there you are, m' dear! (*To Eamonn*) One moment. (*He crosses to Peggy and speaks in a low voice.*) New under-gardener. Needs careful handling.

(*Peggy raises her eyebrows and looks at Eamonn.*)

Sir Henry: (*to Eamonn*) My man, this is Miss Quin.

(*Eamonn is delighted to see someone sane.*)

Eamonn: Ah, how d'you do, Miss Quin. I can't tell you how relieved I am to see you.

(*He holds out his hand. Peggy looks astonished, but takes it.*)

Eamonn: (*in her ear*) I've had an awful time with the old geezer.

Peggy: (*sharply*) I don't understand you.

Eamonn: If he was put in a home, they have some very good injections these days.

Peggy: Will you please start work at once.

Eamonn: (*surprised*) Certainly. Where?

Peggy: In the turnip field beyond the garden.

Eamonn: Won't it be rather chilly later?

Peggy: Not if you put your back into it.

Eamonn: I'd better get my kit.

Peggy: Never mind that. Murphy will give you a spade.

Eamonn: (*to himself*) Another!

Sir Henry: Now what are you hesitating about?

Eamonn: Look here, is this a practical joke.

Peggy: You're the new under-gardener who was coming today, aren't you?

Eamonn: Now I begin to see . . .

(*He bursts out laughing.*)

Sir Henry: What's the joke, sir?

(*Eamonn checks his laughter and snuffs out his cigarette.*)

Eamonn: Nothing, sir. Beg your pardon, sir.

Peggy: Go down to the lodge and see Murphy.

Eamonn: (*crossing to the French windows*) Certainly, miss. Er — excuse me, who is Murphy?

Peggy: The gardener. Didn't he make arrangements with you?

Eamonn: Of course. The name had slipped my memory.

(*He smiles to himself, and is gone.*)

Peggy: Well, did you ever hear anything like that!

(*She crosses to the windows and looks out.*)

Sir Henry: Masters behaving like men, and men like masters. Confusion everywhere.

Peggy: He was rather handsome.

Sir Henry: Don't let the fellow see you watching him.

Peggy: I thought I saw a tall man with a beard coming up the drive. It's only Chris and someone.

(*She turns round and comes back into the room.*)

Sir Henry: Here's your mother.

(*Mrs Quin enters, left, through the inner door.*)

Mrs Quin: Who was that young man?

Peggy: The new under-gardener.

Mrs Quin: I hope he's a better worker than Murphy. If he's a good worker, he can take Murphy's place.

(*There are voices, right, in the hall.*)

Sir Henry: Chris and Murphy.

(*Chris ushers in Murphy.*)

Chris: (*to Mrs Quin*) Evie never came to the door to answer Murphy's ring when he first arrived.

Mrs Quin: I thought I saw her a few hours ago in the greenhouse — or was it the scullery?

Peggy: I imagined I saw her this morning moving through the shrubbery. Oh no, that was day before yesterday.

Mrs Quin: Mr Murphy, you'll stay with us until the wedding, of course.

Murphy: Thank you, m'am.

Mrs Quin: Here's the subject of the portrait. My daughter, Peggy.

(*Mr Murphy takes a parcel out of his pocket and thrusts it into Peggy's hands.*)

Murphy: A little present, Miss Quin. To mark the happy occasion.
Peggy: Oh Mr Murphy, that is kind of you.
Murphy: From our bargain basement. Electroplate, but as good as silver.

(*Peggy reveals a toast-rack.*)

Peggy: Oh just fancy, a toast-rack!

(*Sir Henry clears his throat and waggles his moustache.*)

Mrs Quin: Just what you needed, dear!
Peggy: Yes indeed. So useful for — for putting toast into.
Murphy: If any of your friends are getting married, Miss Quin, I can let you have repeats of that article at cut-throat prices.
Peggy: Thank you, Mr Murphy.

(*She puts the toast-rack on the table with the rest.*)

Chris: By the way, Murphy, where is the artist?
Murphy: Don't you remember, we left him here with the Colonel.
Peggy: Good Lord! Murphy!

(*All turn round and look at her with surprise.*)

Murphy: Excuse me?
Peggy: Mr Murphy, what does this artist look like?
Murphy: (*carelessly*) Oh, I found him poked down on the quays, living in a single room on ten pounds a week, collecting skin rashes and fleas.
Chris: What!
Murphy: You can't expect 'em out of a bandbox for sixty pounds.
Peggy: (*nodding to Sir Henry*) That's him.
Sir Henry: Him all right.
Mrs Quin: Peggy, what is this mystery?
Peggy: Sir Henry and I thought he was the new under-gardener.
Sir Henry: Sent him down to Murphy in the gate lodge.
Peggy: I thought he'd be tall and have a beard and be forty-seven and a quarter.
Mrs Quin: (*in enormous agitation*) Good heavens, ring for Elvie. Ring for Evie at once. No, I'll go down to the lodge myself. I must apologise. Evie! Evie! He'll be mortally offended. Now keep calm, everyone. There's no good losing our heads. He's probably gone back to Dublin by now. Evie! Evie! Drat that girl! And the

wedding's in a week. Now keep cool, that's the only thing. Evie, Evie, Evie . . .

(*She bustles out, right, through the door into the hall, and her cries fade away into the distance.*)

Peggy: (*anxiously*) I thought that Mr —

Murphy: Eamonn O'Sullivan.

Peggy: — O'Sullivan didn't look very well. Skin rashes, you say?

Murphy: And fleas.

Peggy: Fleas. Really. Well, that can be remedied. All he wants is a little nursing —

Murphy: And washing.

Peggy: (*going towards the wall*) I'll ring for Evie and have his bed made ready at once.

Murphy: No need. He probably hasn't actually got a skin rash. But he lives in a filthy hole.

Peggy: (*pausing*) Oh.

Chris: Murphy, why did you get me a creature like that? You're in business in a big way. Surely you've better connections?

Murphy: You asked for a cheap artist.

Peggy: Chris!

Chris: (*with dignity*) I said: not too expensive. Besides, sixty pounds isn't cheap.

Murphy: For a large oil portrait! Chicken feed, believe me.

Chris: Frankly, I don't believe you. I've been rooked.

(*Murphy draws himself up, conscious of his dignity as a major shareholder in a Limited Liability Company.*)

Murphy: I give you my word as a reputable businessman —

Chris: There's no such thing as a reputable businessman. All successful business is founded on fraud. It consists of suggesting to the man from whom you are buying your goods that they are worse than they are, and to the man to whom you are selling them that they are better.

Murphy: (*becoming normal again*) That's true. But it is necessary to suppress these facts in the interests of the shareholders. In business, if anything can be made to appear in the interests of the shareholders, it becomes ethical. We generally manage to make everything appear in the interests of the shareholders.

Chris: As an extensive shareholder myself, I quite approve.

(*Mrs Quin bustles in again.*)

Mrs Quin: I've sent the gardener's boy running down to the gate lodge. I couldn't find Evie anywhere. Though I did think I caught a glimpse of her down at the cowshed.

Peggy: Why didn't you call her?

Mrs Quin: 'Twas only one of the heifers.

Murphy: Eamonn won't go home. (*He draws a handful of patterns out of his pocket.*) While we're waiting, perhaps I could interest you, Miss Quin, in some summer materials from Belfast. In various shades of orange.

(*Peggy crosses over to look at them. She leafs them over.*)

Peggy: You've a blue one here.

Murphy: Ah, that's from Derry. Apprentice Boy blue.

Sir Henry: Mr Murphy, you're managing director of one of the biggest businesses in Dublin. Do you find it necessary to go round with patterns in your pocket? Excuse my asking.

Murphy: Certainly. It's quite simple. One never knows where one mightn't make a sale.

Sir Henry: But you are in such a big way of business!

Murphy: Big things are built out of little things. It's because I've never turned up my nose at the little things that my business has grown so big.

Sir Henry: So that's the secret of the Belfast man's success!

(*During this conversation, Mrs Quin has been gazing out of the French windows.*)

Mrs Quin: Here comes Mr O'Sullivan. Now we ought all to be especially nice to this young man. If he comes from the background that Mr Murphy says he does, he's bound to feel a bit bashful when he sees us.

(*She goes out, right, into the hall.*)

Peggy: Now be ready, everybody. Here he is.

Mrs Quin: (*off*) Ah, Mr O'Sullivan, a thousand welcomes, as we say in Ireland. Come in! Come in! This way.

(*She enters, followed by Eamonn O'Sullivan. He is totally self composed.*)

Mrs Quin: You'll never forgive us all for a most stupid mistake.

(*Eamonn indicates his clothes and general appearance.*)

Eamonn: Quite understandable.

(*Sir Henry, under the impression that he is putting Eamonn at his ease, speaks in his most affable Officer-Commanding-talking-to-the-men manner.*)

Sir Henry: Not at all, my dear chap, not at all. We all felt — felt that a mistake had been made. You're one of us now, you know.

Mrs Quin: Mr O'Sullivan, this is Colonel Sir Henry Robinson.

Eamonn: Colonel! Sir! Why do you Anglo-Irish always seem to bristle with handles to your name?

Sir Henry: (*mournfully*) Everyone goes for my titles these days. They used to inspire respect, even in subalterns.

Mrs Quin: Tut, tut, Mr O'Sullivan. Sir Henry's family has been in Ireland for three hundred years. And here's the subject of your portrait. My daughter, Peggy.

Eamonn: Very pleased to meet you. I have a present for you. It's a —

Mrs Quin and Peggy: (*together*) Toast-rack.

(*Eamonn looks from one to the other of them in astonishment.*)

Eamonn: — cigarette-case.

(*He hands it to Peggy.*)

Chris: What!

Eamonn: Just — just a piece of Moorish craftmanship. I picked it up in an antique shop.

Peggy: It really is lovely. Now that's what I call an absolutely charming present.

Chris: What does it matter whether nicotine comes out of a cardboard packet or a Moorish cigarette case? Coronary sclerosis feels just the same.

Peggy: Can you forgive me for the way I treated you?

Eamonn: (*indicating his shabby clothes*) That's all right. You're a Socialist, aren't you?

Peggy: Heavens no! Why?

Eamonn: They're always so class conscious.

(*Peggy makes a moue of humorous distress at the Colonel.*)

Eamonn: I got on splendidly with your gardener's daughter.

Peggy: (*jealous*) You don't seem to have wasted your time.

Eamonn: I met her on the drive going down. We had a long conversation.

Peggy: About art, I suppose.

Eamonn: I asked her if she'd be my model. She became — er — charmingly feminine.

Peggy: I can imagine.

Eamonn: I asked her would she like to study painting. She said she had studied men, and that was all that any woman needed to study.

Peggy: It seems that she's a philosopher.

Eamonn: I replied that I should be very glad at any time to assist her in her studies —

Mrs Quin: (*hastily changing the subject*) Mr O'Sullivan, I'm greatly interested in Impressionism and Surrealism. Do you do any Surrealist painting? What do you think of Picasso? What do you think of the future of painting in Ireland?

Eamonn: What's this about Impressionism, Surrealism, ism, ism, ism. I'm a man who paints pictures, not labels. I'm much more influenced by Mr Murphy here, who gets me the commissions that pay my landlady — in exchange for the trifling rake-off of twenty-five per cent —

Murphy: Deductable at the source.

Eamonn: Mr Murphy, I regret to say, doesn't trust me. He doesn't trust anyone. You see, he's a businessman.

(*Murphy nods in approval.*)

Eamonn: As for Picasso, he's a little more than a name to me.

Mrs Quin: (*horrified*) Good gracious me!

Eamonn: You see, I'm very lazy about seeing other people's pictures. I'm much too busy painting my own. And I don't care a brace of pheasants about the future of painting in Ireland; only about the future of my own.

Peggy: (*severely*) You seem to be a very great egotist, Mr O'Sullivan.

Eamonn: That's because I'm a very great artist, Miss Quin. True genius is ruthless, reckless and faithless, recking only of the swift passage of time and its urgent need to be upon its way, keeping faith only with its mysterious tryst with the future.

Murphy: Well, as long as you keep a mysterious tryst with my twenty-five per cent commission —

Mrs Quin: (*shocked*) Mr Murphy, a big businessman like you, so mercenary!

Murphy: My money represents my life, my toil. It is the measure of my achievement.

Mrs Quin: I should have thought you would have liked to relax and enjoy a little ease.

Murphy: Ease and relaxation aren't the best sources of happiness, Mrs Quin.

Chris: You're right. It's physical fitness that counts.

Murphy: No. The sense of creation and power.

Peggy: (*half to herself*) That's true.

(*Suddenly Eamonn speaks. He has been silently studying Peggy.*)

Eamonn: Miss Quin, it will give me the very greatest pleasure to confer on you immortality by painting your portrait.

Peggy: (*taken aback*) Thank you.

Eamonn: But you can hardly call this portrait a wedding present.

Mrs Quin: Not a wedding present?

Peggy: Why ever not?

Sir Henry: What d'ye mean, sir?

Murphy: Are you mad?

Chris: It is a wedding present.

Eamonn: (*indicating Chris*) She'll never marry him.

Mrs Quin: Good gracious me!

Chris: Well, I'll be damned!

Murphy: You're offending a customer.

Sir Henry: Ought to be court-martialled!

Eamonn: She's too good for him. Why — why, she's good enough for me!

Mrs Quin: Well I never!

Chris: Ought to punch his head.

Murphy: He'll ruin me.

Sir Henry: Shot out of hand.

(*In the midst of these exclamations, Peggy and Eamonn stand looking at one another.*)

THE CURTAIN FALLS.

ACT TWO

(*The curtain rises on the same room. The table with the wedding presents has been moved to the right-hand wall to make space for an easel, right centre, and a stool, left centre. Peggy, dressed in tennis clothes and holding a racquet, is sitting on the stool having her portrait painted. Eamonn works at the easel. He is looking distinctly tidier and cleaner. There is a second canvas leaning against the foot of the easel.*)

Eamonn: (*after working in silence for a few moments*) You'll never marry Chris. You don't love him.

Peggy: (*with a short laugh*) You've been saying that for the past week. Tomorrow you'll see.

Eamonn: Tomorrow won't be your wedding day.

Peggy: You've been saying that for the past week.

Eamonn: I'm the man you're going to marry.

Peggy: And you've been saying that for the past week.

Eamonn: All he's good for is to play tennis. The whole seven days I've been here, that's all you two have done — played tennis. Except when you've taken time off to come in here for a sitting.

Peggy: I like tennis.

Eamonn: I like eating and sleeping. But they're not enough.

Peggy: You stood in need of both when you first came here. I've never seen a man improve so much in a week.

Eamonn: So that's why you keep pressing second helpings on me! And insist on having my breakfast sent up to me in bed!

Peggy: What d'you mean?

Eamonn: You're falling for me. Admit it.

Peggy: The vanity of men! You show the slightest concern for them, and they think —

Eamonn: So it was only concern for my health?
Peggy: Well, after Mr Murphy's alarming description of you as having skin infections and —
Eamonn: And?
Peggy: And — other things.
Eamonn: I'm as healthy as an ox.
Peggy: When you first arrived, I thought you were the most impertinent man I'd ever met.
Eamonn: And now you think I'm the most attractive.
Peggy: No. The pluckiest.

(*Eamonn laughs.*)

Peggy: You haven't had many chances. Your cocksureness is just your way of keeping your end up.
Eamonn: (*reflectively*) Curious, when a girl starts falling in love with a man, she always at the same time starts canonising him.
Peggy: (*reflectively*) Curious, when a man wants a girl to fall in love with him, and she refuses to do so, he always tries to uphold his masculine superiority by levelling sarcasms at her.

(*Eamonn holds out the handle of his brush at arm's length and measures her with it for the purposes of the portrait.*)

Eamonn: I'm not surprised you fell for me. For one thing, I'm very good-looking.
Peggy: What's the other reason for my infatuation?
Eamonn: I'm your type.
Peggy: Oh.
Eamonn: Helpless. I need looking after. I need second helpings and breakfast in bed.
Peggy: I see.
Eamonn: How can you hope to resist a man who needs breakfast in bed?
Peggy: Not a chance. I see that.
Eamonn: Chris will never need breakfast in bed. That's his undoing.
Peggy: Poor Chris! Oughtn't someone to tell him?
Eamonn: No use. You're either born to have breakfast in bed, or you're not.
Peggy: So I'm fated to leave Chris for you?
Eamonn: It's in the stars. Or, rather, the bacon and eggs.

Peggy: Where will you take me?

Eamonn: To Dublin, naturally. It's the only possible place in which to lead an intelligent life. The rest of Ireland is fit only for pig and poultry breeders.

Peggy: It seems that the intellectuals can't get on without their bacon and eggs. How will you support me?

Eamonn: You have money, haven't you?

Peggy: A great deal.

Eamonn: Then I propose to live on you.

Peggy: Definitely not.

Eamonn: You ought to be delighted to have the honour of supporting, in his early years, one of the great artists of the world.

Peggy: At great personal sacrifice, I decline the offer.

Eamonn: Then there's nothing for it except to get Chris to pay me today the sixty pounds for your portrait.

Peggy: So I'm to allow you first to paint Chris's wedding present to me, and then proceed to use the money he gives you for it to deprive him of his wedding?

Eamonn: He's not *giving* me sixty pounds. I've earned it.

Peggy: How are you going to take me to Dublin?

Eamonn: I told Mulcahy down at the garage that I might need a car.

Peggy: You — you anticipated I might consent to go with you?

Eamonn: Well... Chris and you can't marry. You know one another too well.

Peggy: All married couples eventually know one another too well. Ours will simply be a marriage without the honeymoon.

Eamonn: It's your mother really, isn't it? You could no more snatch this marriage from her, than you could snatch a toy from a child.

Peggy: You think Mother childish?

Eamonn: Childlike. She's imposed upon you the unshakeable tyranny of trust.

Peggy: (*looking out through the French windows*) Here she comes! I suppose to make her usual inspection of the portrait.

Eamonn: What does she know about painting!

Peggy: That's not very gracious of you, seeing that she's done nothing but stand in awe before your pictures.

Eamonn: An artist prefers the company of a real woman, not a collector of artistic tag phrases.
Peggy: What's your idea of a real woman?
Eamonn: She's gentleness, tender-heartedness. She's what a man may put on a pedestal to worship. She may not be well born. She may not even be —
Peggy: She may not be well born! You wouldn't, by any chance, have put Norah on your pedestal?
Eamonn: Who's Norah?
Peggy: You wouldn't of course know that Norah's the name of our gardener's daughter. Who impressed you so much on the drive your first day.
Eamonn: How could I remember —
Peggy: You've only been seeing her regularly.
Eamonn: When? Where?
Peggy: You've been down to the dances at the Scala most nights.
Eamonn: Well?
Peggy: Of course it will come as a great surprise to you to learn that Norah has also been there.
Eamonn: You seem to take a great interest in my activities.
Peggy: (*assuming indifference*) Just mildly amused.

(*She wanders over to the easel.*)

Eamonn: I believe . . .
Peggy: Well?
Eamonn: (*smiling to himself*) Nothing. (*Pause.*) She's a nice girl.

(*He watches her out of the corner of his eye.*)

Peggy: I'm sure she looks very piquant on a pedestal.

(*She picks up the canvas leaning against the foot of the easel.*)

Eamonn: She dances very well.
Peggy: Really? (*She indicates the picture.*) What's this supposed to be?
Eamonn: That's the field with the cattle in it. Near the orchard.
Peggy: It might as well be . . . I suppose I'm just too lowbrow.
Eamonn: It was a failure. One of the worst I've done.

(*Peggy points to the Indian ornament standing on the small table.*)

Peggy: That's my idea of beauty.

Eamonn: (*crossing to it*) Indian?
Peggy: The Colonel gave it to Mother.

(*Eamonn picks it up and examines it.*)

Eamonn: Yes. It is beautiful.
Peggy: Be careful! Worth fifty pounds.
Eamonn: Fifty pounds, eh!

(*He sets it down carefully.*)
(*Mrs Quin enters through the French windows.*)

Mrs Quin: (*to Peggy*) Chris asked me to send you out to play tennis, dear.

(*Peggy makes a moue of distaste.*)

Eamonn: Mrs Quin, Peggy and I —
Peggy: (*sharply*) Eamonn!
Mrs Quin: What is it, Eamonn?
Eamonn: Nothing.
Mrs Quin: Now, Peggy, dear Chris is waiting.
Peggy: Well, let dear Chris . . . (*She controls herself.*) Here you are, Michaelangelo.

(*She pushes the canvas petulantly into Eamonn's hands.*)

Eamonn: Hey, the paint's still wet!
Peggy: What matter.
Eamonn: Might sell it.
Peggy: That! What for?
Eamonn: Oh, I don't know. Perhaps, say, the price of a taxi . . .

(*Peggy walks across to the French windows, giving her mother a kiss on the way. At the windows, she pauses. She looks at Eamonn from behind her mother's back, tosses her head at him, and goes out.*)
(*Mrs Quin has been looking at the portrait on the easel. She laughs indulgently.*)

Mrs Quin: Poor old Peggy! When it comes to art, she's no idea where she is.
Eamonn: Pathetic, isn't it! You have such an acute judgment. What d'you think of this?

(*He hands her the canvas he is holding.*)

Eamonn: A very advanced technique.
Mrs Quin: Marvellous!
Eamonn: I knew you'd appreciate it.
Mrs Quin: I see exactly the effect you were striving for.
Eamonn: I was greatly influenced by the Surrealists.
Mrs Quin: (*thrilled*) Your impression of the Colonel playing billiards, is it not?
Eamonn: (*startled, but recovering*) What an eye you have!
Mrs Quin: D'you really mean that, Eamonn?
Eamonn: To prove it, I'm going to give you this picture. It was you, you know, who inspired it.
Mrs Quin: How thrilling!
Eamonn: Damn it! I forgot!
Mrs Quin: What is it, dear?
Eamonn: Murphy put twenty pounds on it as a retainer.
Mrs Quin: Oh, how disappointing!
Eamonn: And I've spent the twenty pounds. Otherwise I'd pay him back, and let you have it.
Mrs Quin: Never mind. I'd just as soon have another one.
Eamonn: (*hastily*) That wouldn't be the same thing. You see, Mrs Quin, this was the particular picture you inspired.
Mrs Quin: Of course. An artist's feelings are so delicate. If only I could read your mind!
Eamonn: Perhaps it is better not.
Mrs Quin: Well, if I am not to have the picture —
Eamonn: Tell you what I'll do. No —
Mrs Quin: What?
Eamonn: No. No, no, no.
Mrs Quin: Do go on. Please.
Eamonn: I'm so desperate you should have that picture that, do you know, I'd offer Murphy double if necessary to get it back.
Mrs Quin: Good heavens, I wouldn't dream of letting you.
Eamonn: I will. Only, would you believe it, right now I haven't so much as the price of a taxi on me.
Mrs Quin: Now do make use of me in any way that you can.
Eamonn: (*taking her hand and patting it*) I won't hesitate.
Mrs Quin: Now don't be offended at what I'm going to say —
Eamonn: How could I be?

Mrs Quin: If it will make you happier, I'll put up the twenty pounds myself. (*Hastily*) Oh, just a loan, you understand.

Eamonn: No. No. Positively not.

Mrs Quin: All right. I'm sorry. Forget I said it.

Eamonn: (*hastily*) Well, if you insist.

Mrs Quin: Splendid! I'll let you have it presently. (*She wags an indulgent finger.*) And now, dear boy, what about you and Peggy?

Eamonn: How d'you mean, Mrs Quin?

Mrs Quin: Don't think I haven't eyes in my head. I've seen you looking at her.

Eamonn: She's very hard not to look at.

Mrs Quin: You're a dear, simple, guileless boy, but you've no chance there. She's devoted to dear Chris, as indeed we all are. Their marriage means everything to me.

Eamonn: Did you think I might break it up?

(*Mrs Quin laughs, as at a quaint observation by a favourite child.*)

Mrs Quin: Oh dear! Oh dear, what a boy it is! Oh dear!

Eamonn: (*piqued*) It's not so impossible as all that.

Mrs Quin: (*her mirth growing*) I believe the boy is half serious! Consider her position and your position.

Eamonn: My position is so high and awesome, that you should all be lying stretched out at my feet.

Mrs Quin: (*convulsed*) We, who can trace ourselves back to the ancient earls of Desmond!

Eamonn: You talk to me of your little parochial pedigrees — to me, who am of the lineage of Phideas, of Michaelangelo, of Valesquez and of Renoir!

Mrs Quin: (*becoming more serious*) What a boy! You say you are a genius of the future. I'm sure you are. But how can we be quite positive?

Eamonn: No man can see his own stomach. But we all know that we have one. Neither can a man be born to greatness, and not be aware of it.

Mrs Quin: (*impressed, but befogged*) What does that mean?

Eamonn: It means that I'm a better man than Chris. (*Pointing out through the French windows*) He's out there now in his little white shorts, looking like a cross between a Greek god and an urchin,

hitting an indiarubber ball with some wood and catgut over a fish-net.
Mrs Quin: (*slightly alarmed*) Oh dear, you make him sound awful!
Eamonn: Mark my words, Mrs Quin, Peggy will find a wedding breakfast inadequate that's composed of a feast of tennis balls. She will find that marriage provides obstacles more formidable than a tennis net, and problems which not even the best executed of backhands can solve.
Mrs Quin: D'you really think so?
Eamonn: Most solemnly I do, Mrs Quin. Just because he's played rugby football at a good school and has a broad back, while my mother couldn't afford to give me enough to eat, that doesn't make him my superior.
Mrs Quin: Perhaps. But what could you give her that he couldn't?
Eamonn: He can give her a good game of singles, but I should be a perfect doubles partner.

(*He walks over to the French windows and looks out.*)

Eamonn: Here comes Chris. (*He looks pleased.*) They seem to have quarrelled.
Mrs Quin: Oh dear, not again!
Eamonn: (*returning*) He's looking furious. And she's sitting by the tennis court all alone.

(*He takes her arm and urges her, left, towards the inner door.*)

Eamonn: Let's slip away. I don't feel like listening to their wrangling.
Mrs Quin: Very well. I'd like to look at some of your other pictures.
Eamonn: There's one I did of the Colonel playing billiards —
Mrs Quin: Another one!
Eamonn: I mean, of the field with the cattle in it, near the orchard. (*Slyly*) And you can pay me the twenty pounds.
Mrs Quin: No. I'd better stop and see Chris.
Eamonn: (*disappointed*) Oh, all right. But not me.

(*He leaves, left, by the inner door. As he does so, Chris enters. He is dressed in white T-shirt and shorts, and carries a tennis racquet.*)

Mrs Quin: What happened, dear?
Chris: (*in a towering temper*) It's Peggy again. She said that she was going to sit for her portrait for only half an hour.

Mrs Quin: Well, dear?

Chris: She was in here an hour and a half.

Mrs Quin: It's just that she's getting interested in the work.

Chris: Or the worker?

Mrs Quin: It's quite natural —

Chris: Can't you see what's going on under your nose?

Mrs Quin: (*huffed*) I can see what's going on under my nose, and your nose, and anybody else's nose, as well as the next. And that's no way to speak to me.

Chris: I didn't think I'd see the day when a creature out of a Dublin gutter would be petted and fawned on in this house —

Mrs Quin: (*very angry*) Don't be a snob.

Chris: I know my own value, and I know yours. Your family, you know, can trace itself back —

Mrs Quin: — to the ancient Earls of Desmond. What of these little parochial pedigrees?

Chris: (*aghast*) Parochial pedigree!

Mrs Quin: He is of the lineage of Phido, of Angelico, of Valise and of Reno.

Chris: Who's Fido?

Mrs Quin: You've never seen your own stomach, have you?

Chris: I suppose not.

Mrs Quin: Eamonn has. That proves he's great.

Chris: What on earth are you talking about?

Mrs Quin: (*severely*) Just because you've played rugby football and have a broad back, that doesn't mean that you'll be able to eat a wedding breakfast of tennis balls.

Chris: (*becoming alarmed*) Are you feeling well, Mrs Quin?

(*Eamonn calls from the next room, left.*)

Eamonn: Mrs Quin, I have a picture to show you.

Mrs Quin: (*moving towards the door*) Coming, Eamonn. (*To Chris*) Of course I'm well. Isn't it possible that a person might sometimes be inspired?

Chris: (*glancing towards the door*) I think I know the source of your inspiration.

Mrs Quin: Really!

(*With an indignant glance at him, she goes out. Peggy, who has approached unobserved, quietly enters the room by the open French windows. She is carrying her handbag. She speaks in a subdued tone.*)

Peggy: I heard you being rude to Mother.

Chris: Oh, you there!

Peggy: You talked to her as though she were an idiotic child.

Chris: She's behaving like one.

Peggy: Chris, I will not have it.

Chris: I simply told her what I suspected.

Peggy: Oh, and what do you suspect?

Chris: That this Eamonn has been putting his notions into her head. They've just been plotting against me.

Peggy: Mother plotting! And against you! (*She fumbles in her bag.*) Chris, I'm not going to quarrel with you. I'm trying to keep myself calm. (*She takes out the cigarette case which Eamonn had given her.*) You must think what you like about Mother. (*She extracts a cigarette and lights it with trembling fingers.*)

Chris: That's the cigarette case he gave you, isn't it?

(*She replaces the case in her bag without answering. He crosses to her.*)

Chris: Didn't I tell you that you were not to smoke?

(*She draws on the cigarette. There is nothing defiant in the gesture; she is merely struggling not to burst into tears.*)

Chris: Put that cigarette out.

Peggy: (*In a subdued tone*) No, Chris, I'm not going to put it out.

(*He tries to snatch it out of her hand. She turns away. He seizes her arm and twists it behind her back.*)

Peggy: Chris, let me go. I won't be treated like this. Let me go.

(*She is half weeping with frustration and fury.*)

Chris: I'll show you!

(*He takes the cigarette from her, rushes to the French windows, and hurls it out.*)

Peggy: You — bully!

(*Eamonn enters hurriedly.*)

Chris: Get back to your Dublin gutter before I break you in half.

Peggy: You ought to be happy now. You've got a second person to bully.

(*Eamonn, while not daring to challenge the muscular might of Chris, stands his ground.*)

Chris: Go on. Get out of this. And take your portrait with you.

Peggy: That's right! Bully us all!

Chris: (*after a furious glance at Peggy*) My God!

(*He turns abruptly and strides out of the room by the French windows. Eamonn crosses to Peggy.*)

Eamonn: Never mind, Pegtops.

(*Peggy responds by a fresh outburst of weeping. He puts his arm about her shoulders, and she leans her head against him. He produces a handkerchief, which she accepts. She dabs at her eyes.*)

Peggy: He can't treat me like that!

Eamonn: I know.

Peggy: The big clown! (*She dabs.*) Just because we sometimes scrapped as children, he thinks he can go on doing it. (*A dab.*)

Eamonn: Cheer up, Peggy.

Peggy: (*shaking her head*) I can't, Eamonn. I can't.

Eamonn: Here, give me your bag.

(*She yields it up to him. He peers into it.*)

Eamonn: (*delighted*) Oh, you carry my cigarette case with you!

Peggy: It's beautiful!

(*He extracts the case and opens it. She allows him to put a cigarette between her lips.*)

Eamonn: There! That's better, isn't it?

(*He replaces the case in the bag, which he returns to her. He slaps his palm against his side pocket.*)

Eamonn: Matches! Matches! Ah, there they are!

(*He lights her cigarette. For a moment she stands drawing at it, calming herself.*)

Peggy: (quietly) Eamonn, will you marry me?

Eamonn: Are — are you serious?

Peggy: Take me with you to Dublin.
Eamonn: Pegtops, darling, of course. Only —
Peggy: I won't marry him. I will not marry him.
Eamonn: I still can't believe you mean it. I haven't a bean.
Peggy: I'll show you if I mean it!

(*She puts her arm round his neck and kisses him.*)

Eamonn: I say, you don't do things by halves, do you?

(*He kisses her.*)
(*Mrs Quin is heard calling from the next room, left.*)

Mrs Quin: Peggy! Is that you?
Peggy: (*breaking away*) There's Mother!
Mrs Quin: (*nearer*) Peggy!
Peggy: (*to Eamonn*) Quick!

(*She takes up her pose for the portrait, but continues to smoke. Eamonn has barely picked up his brush and placed himself in front of his easel, when Mrs Quin enters holding a hat.*)

Mrs Quin: So you decided against tennis after all! Look, your going-away hat, just arrived from Dublin.

(*Peggy glances uncomfortably at Eamonn.*)

Peggy: It's very nice, Mother.
Mrs Quin: Nice! Is that all you can say?
Peggy: Well, I mean, couldn't we discuss it later?
Mrs Quin: Why, you silly child, you're behaving more like a woman about to be executed than about to be married. Though, indeed, your poor father used to say that it amounted to much the same thing.
Eamonn: I'm sure that Peggy will be much too sensible to allow herself to be executed, Mrs Quin.
Mrs Quin: (*befogged*) What? (*To Peggy*) You don't propose to go away without a hat, do you?
Peggy: No. I suppose not.
Mrs Quin: You *suppose* not! (*She hands her the hat.*) Try it on.

(*Peggy stubs out her cigarette and goes to the mirror.*)

Eamonn: (*sharply*) There's such a thing as putting on the wrong hat.
Mrs Quin: Good gracious me, one can always change it.
Eamonn: Not this hat.

Mrs Quin: Well, of course, it's too late now. But she wouldn't want to change it. We both chose it most carefully.

Eamonn: Some women go right through their lives wearing the wrong hat.

Mrs Quin: They lack taste.

Eamonn: (looking at Peggy) Or perhaps the courage to change it.

Mrs Quin: I never knew you were so interested in hats, Eamonn.

Eamonn: I'm an artist, Mrs Quin. I can tell you a great deal about them. There are the hats of good wives and mothers, shopping hats, cooker-scrubbing hats, but hats looking for romance. There are smart deceitful little hats, hats that can steer their way through an intrigue as skilfully as a mariner his vessel through reefs, but hats that are empty —

Peggy: (*turning round*) And what about my hat?

Eamonn: It's a hat of indecision and make-do. It's a desolate hat.

(*She whips it off and hands it back to her mother. Mrs Quin moves left, towards the inner door.*)

Mrs Quin: (*to Eamonn*) For myself, I like something absolutely plain — only of course in nice bright cheerful colours, with perhaps a few bunches of artificial flowers and fruit clustered thickly round the crown, and plenty of veiling. Well, I must be off.

(*She leaves.*)

Peggy: I can't go, Eamonn.

Eamonn: Peggy —

Peggy: I must have been mad! It was the quarrel with Chris.

Eamonn: So I only caught you on the rebound!

Peggy: No, Eamonn. It's just — none of us can live to ourselves alone.

Eamonn: If you come away and marry me, your mother is certainly going to be upset —

Peggy: There you are, then.

Eamonn: — for a week. Then she'll come round.

Peggy: If I could be sure . . .

(*He moves towards the telephone, drawing her by the hand after him.*)

Eamonn: She will, Peggy. She will. I'm going to ring for a taxi.

Peggy: No.
Eamonn: We must slip away at once.

(*He lifts the receiver.*)

Peggy: I wish someone would tell me why I am doing this.
Eamonn: A kiss to seal the bargain. (*He kisses her.*) Hello. Hello. Will you give me Mulcahy's garage, please. (*He thrusts the receiver into her hand.*) Here, you speak to him. He'll know your voice.

(*Peggy replaces the receiver.*)

Eamonn: Why did you do that?
Peggy: I can't go in these clothes.
Eamonn: Slip upstairs and change them.

(*He urges her towards the inner door, left.*)

Peggy: Mother will see me.
Eamonn: What matter? Walk up the stairs naturally.
Peggy: I won't be five minutes.

(*She is gone.*)

Eamonn: These women!

(*A pretty girl has appeared at the French windows. On catching sight of Eamonn, she draws back, but not before he has seen her.*)

Eamonn: Who's there?

(*He crosses quickly to the windows and looks out.*)

Eamonn: It's Norah, isn't it?

(*He goes out, and returns dragging the unwilling Norah by the hand.*)

Norah: I can't come in here.
Eamonn: Because you're the gardener's daughter? Shame on you, Norah! Where's your democratic spirit? Aren't you as good as any of them?
Norah: Faith, I am that. My dad sent me to two smart schools in Dublin.
Eamonn: *Two* smart schools!
Norah: I was reared in Rathgar and finished in Phibsboro'.
Eamonn: Reared in Rathgar!

Norah: And finished in Phibsboro'. But I'll get my dad into trouble. The mistress says he's bone idle.
Eamonn: Is he?
Norah: (*laughing*) He is.
Eamonn: What are you doing up here?
Norah: I — I had a message for the mistress from Dad.
Eamonn: I was admiring your dancing down at the Scala last night.
Norah: Why don't you ever dance yourself?
Eamonn: I'm no dancer, Norah.
Norah: (*flirtatiously*) There are a lot of girls there would like to dance with you.
Eamonn: Would you dance with me?
Norah: I would, if you asked me.
Eamonn: Ah, it's better for me to stick to my sketching.
Norah: Is that what you do the whole evening, sitting in that corner — sketch?

(*Eamonn nods. He speaks casually.*)

Eamonn: By the way, did you — er — mention anything to Miss Peggy about — er — these dances at the Scala?
Norah: Sure, when does she ever speak to me! Why?
Eamonn: Nothing.
Norah: (*with a flash of daring*) She wasn't jealous of you?
Eamonn: Why d'you say that?
Norah: There's a lot of gossip. You won't be offended . . .
Eamonn: Go on.
Norah: They say you're very keen on her.
Eamonn: They do, do they!
Norah: Aren't you the foolish man, to lose your heart to a girl that's going to be married tomorrow!
Eamonn: Ah, but perhaps she isn't going to be —

(*He stops abruptly. When Norah speaks, her tone is sharp.*)

Norah: What's that?
Eamonn: I was going to say, perhaps she isn't going to be happy with him.
Norah: (*unconvinced*) Oh.
Eamonn: You seem to be very interested in their marriage.
Norah: (changing face) What do I care!

46

(*Eamonn scrutinises her.*)

Eamonn: As a matter of face, Peggy was jealous. Whom d'you suppose she was jealous of?
Norah: Me?
Eamonn: She thought I went down to the Scala to see you.
Norah: Ssh!
(*She holds up her hand and listens.*)
Eamonn: That will be Peggy.
Norah: I must get out of here.

(*She runs to the French windows, but draws back hurriedly as Mrs Quin's voice is heard.*)

Mrs Quin: (*off stage*) Peggy! Peggy!
Peggy: (*off stage*) Yes, Mother?
Mrs Quin: Where are you going, dear?
Peggy: Just — just for a stroll.
Mrs Quin: Enjoy yourself.

(*Eamonn turns to Norah.*)

Eamonn: You wanted to see Mrs Quin. There she is.
Norah: That's right.

(*But she makes no move to go.*)

Eamonn: Aren't you going?
Norah: Mr Eamonn, don't give me away. There was no message.
Eamonn: Then what —
Norah: I can't say. If Dad loses his job . . . Well, 'tis yourself knows what it is to be poor.
Eamonn: What d'you want me to do?
Norah: Say you forced me to come in. Say it wasn't my fault.
Eamonn: No.
Norah: Sure, it can do you no harm. She's marrying Mr Chris tomorrow.
Eamonn: Suppose . . . I mean, just suppose . . . Quick, out through the front door.
Norah: They can see the drive.
Peggy: (*off stage*) Eamonn!

(*Norah clutches him.*)

47

Norah: Promise!

(*Eamonn points to the window curtains.*)

Eamonn: Hide there.

(*She runs and hides behind the left-hand curtain. As she does so, Peggy enters. She has changed into a summer dress and carries a large shoulder bag. She glances round the room.*)

Peggy: Was there anyone here?
Eamonn: Who should there be? Quick! Let's go.

(*He takes her arm and tries to hurry her towards the hall and front door, right. Peggy resists.*)

Peggy: I thought I heard voices.
Eamonn: Hurry. I hear someone coming. (*He glances at the curtain.*) I mean, we don't want your mother to stop us from (*he glances again at the curtain*) — from going out for a stroll.
Peggy: Stroll?

(*Eamonn glances at the curtain.*)

Eamonn: Well, you know . . . Whatever you like to call it.

(*Peggy has followed his glance. She walks over to the windows.*)

Peggy: I generally like to call a thing by its name. Unless there's a good reason for not doing so.
Eamonn: Where are you going?
Peggy: I saw the gardener's cat outside the window. Funny, I've never seen him up here before.
Eamonn: Never mind.

(*She rests her hand on the curtain behind which Norah is concealed, and looks out.*)

Peggy: Except once when he followed up Norah from the lodge. He's run up the creeper. The poor thing seems to be caught behind some wire netting.

(*She goes just outside the windows to free the cat.*)

Eamonn: Peggy, don't mind him. Let's get away for our — walk.
Peggy: (*still outside*) Elopement, darling, elopement. (*She re-enters and speaks with satisfaction.*) There, I've let the cat out!

(*Eamonn glances at the curtain.*)

Eamonn: I can't argue with that.

(*There is a sneeze behind the curtain.*)

Peggy: What was that?

Eamonn: I didn't hear anything.

Peggy: I heard a sneeze.

Eamonn: Oh, that! It was only the cat.

Peggy: Why should the cat sneeze?

Eamonn: He's got a cold. He — he was out late last night.

Peggy: How d'you know?

Eamonn: (*desperately*) He — he was down at the Scala.

Peggy: What was he doing there?

Eamonn: (*on the point of giving up*) How should I know? He wasn't dancing.

(*Nora puts him out of his misery by slowly emerging.*)

Peggy: Norah! What are you doing in there?

Norah: He made me come in, Miss Peggy. He dragged me in. Wasn't that it, Mr Eamonn?

(*Eamonn, after reading the appeal in Norah's eyes a moment, shrugs his shoulders.*)

Eamonn: Yes. Yes, it was I made her come in.

Peggy: (*bitterly*) It seems I ought to take up dancing at the Scala. Telling me what you did to my face, and all the time behind my back . . .

(*Eamonn remains silent.*)

Peggy: (*in a blaze of anger*) There isn't a shred of decent feeling in you. I should have listened to Chris. 'Dublin gutter,' that's what he called you.

(*She abruptly leaves by the inner door, left. Norah catches Eamonn by the sleeve.*)

Norah: You're — you're a gentleman!

Eamonn: Peggy!

(*He pulls his arm away, and follows after her. Footsteps approach from the garden.*)

Norah: Lawks, there's someone coming!

(*She conceals herself behind the same curtain. Chris enters through the French windows.*)

Chris: Peggy! Peggy!
Norah: (*emerging*) Hello, Chris!
Chris: Good Lord! Norah! I told you never to come up here.
Norah: Afraid I might spoil your wedding?
Chris: You're not going to make trouble for me?
Norah: Maybe.
Chris: Just because I — I flirted with you a little!
Norah: I'm going to have a baby.
Chris: Impossible!
Norah: It's been done before. That's what comes of — flirting.
Chris: Think of my position!
Norah: Think of mine. My family has always kept itself respectable. If we've ever had anything to be ashamed of, we've always done the proper thing, and hushed it up.
Chris: Well, money can hush up anything.
Norah: And marriage can hush up more.
Chris: I can't marry you.
Norah: You're a gentleman, and I'm not. I told my Da it was no use.
Chris: He knows?
Norah: He said, if I couldn't get marriage out of it, what was the use of sweating his guts out to send me to two smart schools in Dublin.
Chris: Good Lord!
Norah: I was reared in Rathgar and finished in Phibsboto'.

(*Chris has begun striding up and down.*)

Chris: I've got to think of my position. I owe it to myself. At the cost of any self-sacrifice, I must not let myself down.

(*He pauses in front of her.*)

Chris: Is there anybody else would marry you? I'd make it worth his while.
Norah: I'd have to know, there's plenty would have married me in Phibsboro'. And they wouldn't have wanted money either.
Chris: I know. I know.

Norah: I'd have you know, there was one chap mad to give me the ring. Very respectable — in the Gas, Light and Coke Company. I'd have you know —

Chris: I know. I know. But we haven't any gas or coke here. I was thinking of a young farmer.

Norah: I wouldn't fancy a farmer.

Chris: What's wrong with a farmer?

Norah: The odours about a farmhouse is not very savoury.

Chris: What about the odour of gas? Anyway, they're all farmers around here.

Norah: Not all.

Chris: Who?

Norah: There's an artist . . .

Chris: Are you mad? What do all you women see in him? He can't expand his chest even two inches.

Norah: He's a real gentleman.

Chris: (*resuming his pacing*) It might work at that. He'd do anything for money.

Norah: Maybe not this.

Chris: (*aghast*) Not even for *money*?

(*Norah shakes her head.*)

Chris: Good Lord, is there no decency left!

(*An idea strikes him.*) Say he's the father.

Norah: In a week?

Chris: Don't mention to anyone you're — you're the way you are. Just tell the mistress he promised to marry you.

(*Norah shakes her head.*)

Norah: He was very decent to me.

Chris: In your position, you can't afford to be too delicate.

Norah: You're very hard.

Chris: I have to think of my position. A position is like a physique; it needs keeping up by daily exercise. I'll fetch Mrs Quin, and you must tell her he promised to marry you.

Norah: (*reflectively*) He told me that Miss Peggy thought he was going down to the dance every night to see me.

Chris: That makes it easy. Mrs Quin will chuck him out of the house.

Things will be all right again between Peggy and me.
Norah: So that's all you're thinking about?
Chris: I'm paying good money to fix you up, aren't I? With him or, if that fails, with some other husband. Now wait here. I'll fetch Mrs Quin. She's out in the garden with the Colonel.

(*He goes out by the French windows.*)

Norah: (*to herself*) They wouldn't have wanted money in Phibsboro'. There was one chap who put eau de quinine on his hair. He smelt lovely. A sanitary inspector.

(*Voices and footsteps approach from the inner room, left.*)

Norah: Lawks!

(*She hides behind the curtain.*)

Eamonn: (*off*) I tell you, Peggy, it's just as I said. I promise you.
Peggy: (*off*) You and your promises!

(*Eamonn enters the sitting-room. Peggy follows him, still wearing her shoulder bag.*

Eamonn: I had to help her out. Ask her yourself.
Peggy: I will.
Eamonn: (*looking round the room*) She's gone!
Peggy: Just as I thought.
Eamonn: Peggy, I swear it!

(*He runs over to the French windows and looks out. He returns disconsolately.*)

Eamonn: She's gone all right. I'm beaten. You must believe what you like.

(*There is a pause.*)

Peggy: Eamonn.
Eamonn: Yes?
Peggy: I'd like to believe you.
(*He takes her hand and speaks quietly.*)
Eamonn: You can, darling.
Peggy: You're such a rascal! But then, I suppose all men are.
Eamonn: We are, Peggy, we are. We all need watching.
Peggy: Can a girl never relax?

Eamonn: Never. It's the price of love. (*He kisses her.*) Let's phone Mulcahy.

(*He takes her hand and leads her across to the telephone. On the way, he looks at the shoulder bag.*)

Eamonn: Will you have enough there?

Peggy: We can't walk away from the house bowed down under suitcases. What about yourself?

(*Eamonn lifts the receiver, listens a moment, then puts it into her hand.*)

Eamonn: What did I have when I came here? I'll buy a toothbrush.

(*He wanders across to the small table on which stands the bric-a-brac, including the Indian ornament.*)

Peggy: (*into the telephone*) Hello. Hello.

(*Eamonn picks up the Indian ornament and examines it.*)

Eamonn: Worth fifty pounds, you said?

Peggy: (*not hearing him*) Hello! Is that Mulcahy's?

(*Eamonn slips the ornament into his pocket.*)

Peggy: Oh, Mr Mulcahy, this is Miss Quin speaking. Would you send up a car at once. Yes. Very urgent. I'll walk down and meet it. Yes. Thank you.

(*As she puts down the receiver. Murphy, who has approached unnoticed, enters the room from the French windows. Eamonn, who has crossed towards Peggy, doesn't see him.*)

Eamonn: Quick, darling, let's get away before anyone comes.

Murphy: (*to himself*) Darling! (*Coming forward; to Eamonn*) One moment!

Eamonn: Oh, you there! (*Suspiciously*) When did you come in?

Murphy: Just in time, I imagine.

Eamonn: (*in a fever to be off*) What is it you want?

Murphy: Mrs Quin tells me that she's just bought a picture.

Eamonn: Well, that's so.

Murphy: You agreed to pay commission on every piece of work you sold while staying here.

Eamonn: I'll — I'll get in touch with you.

(*He pushes Peggy towards the hall.*)

Murphy: The contract says I may deduct my commission at the source. If you don't settle now, I'll sue.

Peggy: Better settle, Eamonn. He's got you.

(*Eamonn comes back sulkily, pulling out some notes.*)

Eamonn: Twenty-five per cent of twenty pounds is four pounds. There!

(*He thrusts the notes into Murphy's hands.*)

Murphy: (*holding out one of his hands*) Five pounds.

(*Eamonn, after glaring at him, yields up the extra pound.*)

Eamonn: Come on, Peggy. That settles him.

(*He pushes her again towards the hall.*)

Murphy: One moment!

Eamonn: Well, what now?

Murphy: Mrs Quin said that you charged her a pound for signing the picture. Twenty-five per cent of a pound is twenty-five pence.

Eamonn: Well, I'm damned if you'll get it.

Murphy: Then I'll sue.

Eamonn: You'd sue a friend for twenty-five pence?

Murphy: I'd sue my grandmother for the price of a cup of hot tea, if she staggered uninvited into my house out of a snow blizzard.

Eamonn: I wonder you find it worth it!

Murphy: (*virtuously*) It's the principle of the thing.

Peggy: I see Chris coming up the garden.

(*Eamonn throws some coins down on the table holding the wedding presents, and hurries Peggy out through the door, right. He has almost disappeared himself, when Murphy, who has been examining a coin, calls him back.*)

Murphy: Just a second!

(*Eamonn reappears.*)

Murphy: This is a foreign coin.

Chris: (*off*) Peggy! Peggy!

(*Peggy peers back into the room from the hall.*)

Peggy: Eamonn, come on.

(*Eamonn pulls out a coin and flings it full at Murphy's head, then leaves.*)

Murphy: You wouldn't see that in Belfast! Typical Dublin behaviour!

(*He gropes after the coin, recovers it, holds it up to the light, tests it between his teeth, and drops it into his pocket. He rises to his feet and gazes at the portrait.*)

Murphy: Taxi to meet them! And the portrait isn't finished!
Chris: (*off*) Peggy!
Murphy: Suppose Chris doesn't pay me! I must get the money before . . .

(*Chris enters and, on seeing Murphy, sweeps his gaze round the room.*)

Chris: Hello, Murphy! Er — when you came in — you didn't see — anyone?
Murphy: Oh, there you are! I've come to ask you — about this portrait — don't want to rush you, but I may have to go up to Belfast tomorrow . . .
Chris: My cheque? Certainly. This evening. Have you seen Mrs Quin or Peggy?
Murphy: Peggy? Yes, she was in here a moment ago. Forgive me, but I may have to travel up to Belfast today.
Chris: (*impatiently*) Certainly. Certainly. In an hour or so. She was here, you say?
Murphy: With Eamonn. But excuse me. I may have to be off to Belfast positively at once.

(*Chris plucks out his cheque book.*)

Chris: Have you got a pen?

(*Murphy has his pen out in a flash.*)

Murphy: Forgive me. Don't want to rush you. There's no hurry at all. Thanks awfully.

(*Chris scribbles out a cheque.*)

Chris: Which way did they leave?
Murphy: Out through the front door. (*He takes the cheque.*) Thanks awfully. I think they were going for a stroll. (*He moves towards*

the inner door, left.) Well, perhaps I ought to be packing.
Chris: Where's Mrs Quin?
Murphy: In the greenhouse.

(*He leaves by the inner door, left. Norah at once emerges.*)

Chris: Can't you stop bobbing out from behind that curtain!
Norah: Chris, 'tis no stroll they've gone for. They've eloped.
Chris: Good Lord!

(*He rushes to the French windows.*)

Chris: Mrs Quin! Mrs Quin! Sir Henry!
Mrs Quin: (*off*) What is it, dear?
Chris: Come here quickly.
Norah: You'll have to marry me now.

(*Chris has begun to stride up and down.*)

Chris: Don't talk nonsense.
Norah: There was a very smart chap in Phibsboro' —
Chris: I'm trying to think.
Norah: Used eau de quinine —
Chris: For heaven's sake! Listen. I'm going to follow them. I'll get the others to come too. When I find them, I'll phone you at the lodge. You come at once. Take a taxi. Then accuse Eamonn of breach of promise.
Mrs Quin: (*off*) What can have happened, Colonel? It's not like Chris. Evie! Evie!
Sir Henry: (*off*) Steady, girl, steady. Always stay steady under fire.
Chris: Quick! Out by the front door! Remember, taxi, breach of promise.

(*He pushes her into the hall, right. Mrs Quin and Sir Henry enter.*)

Chris: Peggy and Eamonn have eloped.
Sir Henry: No! Ought to be shot!
Mrs Quin: The poor romantic darling!
Chris: Romantic! What a rotten way to treat me — I, who have done everything for her. Given her a start of thirty points in every game and never served my hardest.
Sir Henry: Fellow's a bounder, running off with a girl above his station.

Mrs Quin: She should have told me. She must have gone off without half her things. And she has a delicate chest. Evie! Evie!

(*Murphy enters calmly.*)

Murphy: And he knew that I had several more commissions lined up for him in the neighbourhood.

Chris: You can talk about business at a time like this!

Murphy: What else is there to talk about at any time?

Mrs Quin: Where can they have gone?

Murphy: He's probably taken her to his room in Dublin.

Chris: I'm going to bring her back, if I've got to knock him down to do it.

Sir Henry: Better be careful of assault, old man. I'll come with you.

Chris: Thanks, Colonel.

(*Chris goes to the phone.*)

Mrs Quin: I'll pack some of her clothes and come with you. Oh dear, I hope there won't be a horrible scene.

(*Chris pauses on his way to the phone. He speaks to her reassuringly.*)

Chris: There won't be any scene at all, Mrs Quin. I'll knock him out with the first punch. (*Into the phone*) Hello. Hello. Would you give me Mulcahy's, please.

Murphy: I suppose I'd better be there to pick up my client.

Mrs Quin: (*to herself*) There's her picture hat and her pink panties. Evie! Evie! Drat that girl!

Sir Henry: D'you remember, we saw her this morning, slipping down between the rows of scarlet runners?

Mrs Quin: No, that was the gardener's boy.

Sir Henry: By Jove, yes. And it was last week.

Mrs Quin: (*to herself*) She'll want her scent.

Chris: Is that you, Mr Mulcahy?

Mrs Quin: (*to herself*) There's that bottle of Kashmiri Moonlight from Rafferty's Pharmacy in Ballydehob.

Chris: (*into the phone*) Would you please send up a car at once to Mrs Quin's house. Yes. Yes.

Mrs Quin: (*to herself*) Or the Southern Surrender she got from that Orangeman in Belfast.

Chris: (*into the phone*) Send up the largest car you have.

Mrs Quin: (to herself) Oh dear, oh dear, I don't know what I'll do if I find she's being starved.

Chris: (*into the phone*) I should fill her up with petrol.

Mrs Quin: One minute I could cry —

Chris: (*into the phone*) And fill up the radiator.

Mrs Quin: — and the next I'm so angry, I could put her over my knee and spank her.

Chris: (*into the phone*) I should certainly grease her back axle.

Mrs Quin: (*leaving by the inner door, left*) Evie! Evie! Evie!

Chris: (*into the phone*) There'll be a big party travelling. For a wedding? No. No. (*He bangs down the receiver.*) But there may be a funeral.

CURTAIN

ACT THREE

(*The curtain rises on a shabby lodging-house room, in extreme contrast to the prosperous comfort of Mrs Quin's sitting-room. There is a window in the back wall, through which may be seen the roof-tops of a small country town. A door in the right-hand wall [the inner door] leads to an annex [unseen]. One in the left-hand wall [the outer door] leads to a landing [unseen], reached by a staircase from the lower storeys of the house. In the back right-hand corner of the room is a gas ring, a working surface and a sink. Peggy is boiling a kettle. A bed occupies the centre of the wall. Nearby hangs a picture of Eamonn's, a Crucifixion. There are two chairs and a folding table, the latter leaning against the wall. Near the outer door, left, stands an easel with a painting on it. It is early evening.*)

Eamonn is reading from a notice on the wall.)
Eamonn: Listen to this, darling. (*He reads.*) All electricity will be switched off at midnight. (*He turns to Peggy.*) Is there anything quite as impertinent as boarding-house rules?
Peggy: I don't know, darling. I've never been in a boarding-house before.
Eamonn: (*reading*) Rent, in advance, is to be paid regularly by the week. (*He turns to Peggy.*) Suppose one paid it irregularly? Crept down the stairs naked at midnight, woke up the landlady, and insisted on paying her in Spanish money?
Peggy: Definitely against the rules.
Eamonn: Even if one wore a loincloth and a sombrero?
Peggy: Even so.
Eamonn: Life is very hard. (*He crosses to her.*) I'm head over heels in love with you, Pegtops.
Peggy: You've already given your heart away to someone else.

Eamonn: Who?

Peggy: To a certain Eamonn O'Sullivan, your first love and your last.

Eamonn: You're very unfair to me, Peggy.

Peggy: Now don't sulk!

(*He keeps his face averted. She puts her arms round his neck.*)

Peggy: Nearly brought disaster on us, didn't you? Going back to the house like that to fetch away your pictures! But I'm glad I eloped with you.

Eamonn: (*softening*) Are you, Pegtops?

(*He tries to kiss her. She draws back but smiles at him.*)

Peggy: Now don't get a swollen head!

(*Eamonn impatiently breaks down her resistance and draws her to him. He showers kisses on her, and finally she completely yields herself.*)

Peggy: (*pushing him away*) The kettle's boiling. Set up the table.

Eamonn: Never mind the kettle.

Peggy: That's no way to talk about a kettle. Show some respect.

(*She crosses to the gas ring, and he to the folding table which he sets up.*)

Eamonn: What are we having for tea?

Peggy: Pressed beef.

Eamonn: We had pressed beef for lunch. I haven't yet had experience of your breakfast. Does that consist of pressed beef also?

Peggy: Of course.

(*Standing at the working surface, she begins to slice up the beef.*)

Eamonn: What's the time?

Peggy: Seven o'clock.

Eamonn: Seven. And we slipped away at twelve. Just seven hours ago.

Peggy: I wonder how soon they'll find us?

Eamonn: Days, probably. They'll assume that we've gone to my room in Dublin. They'd never dream of looking for us here right in the very neighbourhood.

Peggy: I've only once been in this little town. We always drove the twenty miles to Dublin for our shopping. Think of the sensation when we go to the priest to get married!

(*Eamonn starts, and raises his eyebrows.*)

Eamonn: Married? Oh yes, married. Of course. But I couldn't pass up all those commissions Murphy has got me. I suppose he'll be along for his twenty- five per cent.

Peggy: Fetch me down the tea, darling.

(*Eamonn crosses to a high shelf above the working surface.*)

Eamonn: I believe that man will extract a twenty-five per cent commission from the firm to which he gives out the contract for his own funeral. Which is the tea?

Peggy: In the tin marked 'Sugar'.

Eamonn: Then where's the sugar?

Peggy: Tin marked 'Tea'.

Eamonn: But of course. Ask a silly question . . .

(*He takes down both the tins.*)

Peggy: (*sighing*) Fancy me, a Bohemian! A Bohemian of seven hours standing. Seven hours away from the bourgeois life with its petty conventions, its petty counting of cash, its worship of the sanctity of property. (*She shudders.*) Ough! That awful, 'I own this, and you own that.'

Eamonn: Glad you feel like that about it.

(*He produces the Indian ornament from his pocket and holds it up.*)

Peggy: That's Mother's Indian ornament!

Eamonn: Worth fifty pounds, you said.

Peggy: You rotten thief! Have you no respect for other people's property?

Eamonn: My twenty pounds won't last for ever.

(*Peggy snatches at it.*)

Peggy: Give it to me.

(*Eamonn slips out of her reach and puts down the ornament on the folding table.*)

Eamonn: Remember, it's my duty to support you.
Peggy: Why can't you get a job?
Eamonn: I've no qualifications. I'm good for nothing.

Peggy: Then why not write for the stage? Supper's ready.

(*She ferries the tea etc over to the table.*)

Eamonn: You've left on the ring.

Peggy: I want to boil a kettle of washing-up water after supper.

Eamonn: We'll be half an hour over supper.

Peggy: Only twenty minutes. (*She sits down.*) Now come on, like a good boy!

Eamonn: I'm damned if I'll be a good boy. (*He turns off the gas.*) It would choke me to sit and eat with waste like that going on.

Peggy: I thought you were a Bohemian and didn't think about waste.

(*He sits down.*)

Eamonn: And who else should think more about waste than an artist, the most constructive of men with the least money?

Peggy: You're as bad as Chris. I thought I was escaping from all that.

Eamonn: Chris is quite right.

Peggy: Eamonn, aren't you the most astounding — Ssh!

(*They both listen.*)

Eamonn: It sounds like an army coming up the staircase.

Peggy: You don't suppose . . .

Eamonn: They couldn't have so soon.

Peggy: Go and look.

(*He goes, left, to the outer door and peers out. The sound of tramping and voices grows.*)

Eamonn: (*whispering*) It's them. Hundreds of them.

(*He closes the door hastily.*)

Peggy: Hundreds?

Eamonn: Well, half a dozen at least. Chris looks perfectly furious.

(*The footsteps and voices grow to a crescendo. Then they cease. There is a moment's silence, followed by a loud knocking on the door.*)

Chris's voice: Anyone in?

Peggy: (*whispering*) Answer him.

Eamonn: (*whispering*) No.

Chris's voice: (*more loudly*) Anyone there?

Peggy: (*whispering; but determinedly*) Go on, Eamonn.

(*After a surprised look at the expression on her face, reluctantly he speaks aloud.*)

Eamonn: Yes. That is, I think so.

(*The door is flung open, and the inflamed face of Chris is thrust into the room. He advances, and Eamonn retreats before him. The others enter behind Chris: Mrs Quin, Sir Henry, Murphy carrying a suitcase, and a priest.*)

Chris: (*speaking quietly*) Peggy, Father McMahon is here. He's going to ask you to come home.

Peggy: Good evening, Father.

Father McMahon: Good evening, Peggy.

(*Chris, preserving his quiet tone, addresses himself to Eamonn.*)

Chris: I'm a quiet peaceable chap, and I've come here to abide quietly and absolutely by Peggy's decision and the decisions of the others. (*His voice rises.*) But if she doesn't decide to come home, I'll carry her home by force, and (*shaking his fist under Eamonn's nose*) as for you, you upstart little runt —

(*Mrs Quin slips between them and puts her hands on Chris's arms.*)

Mrs Quin: Chris, dear, better leave this to me.

(*She crosses with affectionate impulsiveness to Peggy. Peggy meets her half way.*)

Mrs Quin: Hello, darling!
Peggy: Hello, Mumsie!

(*They embrace.*)

Mrs Quin: Come home, darling.
Peggy: I can't, Mother. I can't.
Mrs Quin: You weren't happy I know, dear.
Peggy: Such nonsense, Mother! You spoilt me thoroughly.
Mrs Quin: You wanted to do something useful.
Peggy: Yes, I do.
Mrs Quin: We all need you. Chris needs you.
Peggy: (*in a low voice*) I don't love him, Mumsie.
Mrs Quin: Do you . . . Are you happy here?

(*Peggy nods. Mrs Quin reflects a moment.*)

Mrs Quin: Well then, dear, you must stay of course.
Chris: What!
(*Peggy throws her arms round her mother's neck and kisses her.*)
Peggy: Oh Mumsie!
Mrs Quin: Now let's see, you'll want some more clothes. (*To Murphy*) Mr Murphy, thank you for lifting Peggy's suitcase up the stairs.
Murphy: That's all right, m'am.
(*He puts down the suitcase by the wall near the door.*)
Peggy: We'll be married quite quietly. I'll have my nigger-brown costume and hat —
Mrs Quin: Oh no, dear. I think your navy blue is much nicer.
Chris: Look here —
Peggy: What hat, d'you think?
Mrs Quin: Now let me see. I think the one you got at O'Byrne's.
Chris: For heaven's sake —
Peggy: Or what about the little pink and blue one?
(*Chris turns to Father McMahon.*)
Chris: Can't you do something, Father?
Mrs Quin: That's a splendid idea! And your blue suede shoes.
Father McMahon: What! Try to insert a word edgeways between two women talking clothes!
Peggy: Oh no. No, Mother.
Father McMahon: St Peter himself couldn't do it.
Mrs Quin: No. Perhaps they're not really for a smart occasion.
Chris: (*shouting*) Stop it, stop it, stop it!
(*The two women turn and look at him in surprise.*)
Mrs Quin: Chris dear!
Chris: You stand there discussing clothes as though you were gossiping in Grafton Street!
Mrs Quin: But, dear, what else is there to discuss?
Chris: Peggy's return home.
Mrs Quin: Dear! She loves Eamonn.
(*Chris throws up his hands.*)
Chris: Love! 'She loves Eamonn!' And that's that! Love is the be-all and end-all of everything!

Mrs Quin: It makes the world go round.
Chris: It doesn't. It merely makes women's heads go round.

(*Sir Henry steps forward briskly.*)

Sir Henry: Leave this to me, Mrs Quin. Matter for an old soldier. (*To Chris and Eamonn.*) Well, young men, did you see the newspaper this morning?
Eamonn: Which newspaper?
Sir Henry: The 'Irish Times' of course. The editor gives it as his considered opinion that we shall find ourselves involved in open rebellion within a fortnight.
Chris: Is it trouble with the IRA?
Sir Henry: (*impatient with this stupidity*) I'm talking about the natives of Bungawalla. The 'Irish Times' considers that we should send substantial units of the army overseas at once.
Murphy: Sure, if we did that, the Reverend Ian Paisley would be across the Border like a flash.

(*Sir Henry wheels round and stares at him.*)

Sir Henry: I'm talking about *The* Army. The British Army.

(*He turns back to Eamonn and Chris.*)

Sir Henry: Year or so of campaigning abroad would solve the problem for you two.
Chris: It would only postpone it.
Sir Henry: (*with cheerful enthusiasm*) Not at all, dear boy! One of you will probably be killed.
Eamonn: Suppose we're both killed?
Sir Henry: Highly unlikely. At the worst, the one of you who survives may be a little maimed. Perhaps an eye lost, or a leg or an arm gone. But, bless you (*he laughs heartily*), the ladies find such little discrepancies romantic.
Peggy: Thank you, Sir Henry, this lady prefers her man in one piece.
Sir Henry: Very well. Murphy, you supplied the artist. Now you control him.
Chris: Hear, hear!

(*Murphy approaches the table. While speaking, he picks up the Indian ornament and examines it.*)

Murphy: You are under contract to me. I've a lot of commissions lined up for you. I demand that you return to portrait-painting and stop annoying a client.

Eamonn: I didn't sell you myself for twenty-five per cent, you know.

(*Murphy holds up the ornament.*)

Murphy: How much is this worth?

(*Eamonn is in a fever lest Mrs Quin, who is talking in a low voice to Peggy, should see it. He motions to him vigorously to put it away.*)

Murphy: Eh? What's that?

Eamonn: I don't know. Fifty pounds.

(*Murphy puts down the ornament. Chris turns to Father McMahon.*)

Chris: Father, aren't you going to speak to him?

(*Father McMahon comes slowly forward, and all watch him expectantly. He opens his mouth, seems about to speak, then closes it again. He produces a small missionary box from his pocket, which he rattles. He crosses to Mrs Quin.*)

Father McMahon: Will you let me have a little something for the Catholic mission to Bungawalla?

Sir Henry: Bungawalla!

Chris: Collecting for a mission at a time like this!

Mrs Quin: The Catholic Mission to Bungawalla is Father McMahon's pet mission. He'd collect for it at any time.

(*She drops some coins out of her bag into the box. He moves on to Murphy, who reluctantly extracts his wallet.*)

Murphy: Have you change of a pound? I'll give five shillings.

Father McMahon: (*taking the note*) I'll see. (*He folds it up and inserts it into the box without making any attempt to look for change.*) No, I haven't.

(*Murphy makes a grimace of dispair.*)
(*Father McMahon turns at once to Sir Henry.*)

Father McMahon: Colonel?

Sir Henry: Suppose they use the money for machine-guns instead of Masses?

Father McMahon: I hope not. I hope not. But we shall all meet in heaven in any case. Will you subscribe?

Sir Henry: Certainly not. I hope yo *pass* into heaven some day. But I'm damned if I'll be *blown* into it by the Bungawalla Catholic Mission.

Father McMahon: Chris?

Chris: I'll put in a pound, Father. (*He folds up and inserts the note.*) But if you'll talk to this man (*jerking his head towards Eamonn*), I'll write you a cheque for fifty pounds.

Father McMahon: Fair enough.

(*He turns to Eamonn.*)

Father McMahon: Although you're an Englishman, I believe you were brought up a Catholic.

Eamonn: That's right, Father.

Father McMahon: All the same, I don't suppose you'll subscribe to my mission. I didn't see you in chapel on Sunday.

Eamonn: There's nothing to prevent a man who never goes to church from preserving his faith in his own home.

Father McMahon: A true picture-lover doesn't keep away from galleries, merely because he has pictures on his own walls. Neither does a true God-lover keep away from God's house.

Eamonn: You have me there, Father. I'd better come clean. I'm an agnostic.

Sir Henry: An agnostic! But — but an agnostic is a cad!

Eamonn: Yes, Colonel.

Sir Henry: A Roman Catholic is another thing. A Roman Catholic one can almost understand. We had a lot of them of course in the Irish regiments. (*He looks round at the company.*) Quite decent chaps, really, when you got to know them. Of course on Sunday they had their own chaplain and service. But imagine marching off a squad of agnostics on Sunday to — what? Personally, I'd give 'em fatigue duties. There's only one way to deal with an agnostic; make him peel potatoes for the mess for a couple of hours. That would soon put him in a better frame of mind. What d'you say, Father McMahon?

Father McMahon: (*rubbing his chin*) In our various conversions made among the heathen and the atheist, I don't recall any statistics as to the efficacy of peeling potatoes.

(*Chris suddenly loses his last bestige of patience and advances upon Eamonn.*)

Peggy: Look out, Eamonn!

Chris: Put up your fists.

Eamonn: (*recoiling*) Now look here, Chris —

(*Chris strips off his coat.*)

Chris: Put 'em up.

Mrs Quin: Stop them fighting, Father.

(*Father McMahon takes her gently by the arm and draws her back.*)

Father McMahon: There are worse ways, Mrs Quin, of settling things than fisticuffs.

Mrs Quin: Oh dear, this is dreadful! Evie! Evie! Oh no, of course, she isn't here.

Eamonn: (*to Chris*) I'm not such a fool as to play you at your own game, on your own ground.

Chris: So you're a coward as well as a cad!

Peggy: Don't let him taunt you, Eamonn.

Eamonn: Fight a muscle-bound booby like that! It would be playing into his hands.

Peggy: Never mind. But don't let him call you a coward.

Eamonn: You took a different line on the last occasion. What's made you change your mind?

Peggy: I'm a woman.

Eamonn: Tell me, is there some law which permits a woman to change her mind, but forbids a man to do so.

Peggy: Probably not. But there ought to be.

Eamonn: Up to this you've been doing your best to build me up. Now you're doing your best to knock me down.

Peggy: I'm doing it for your own good.

Eamonn: A punch on the jaw will do me good?

Peggy: Yes.

Eamonn: Where's the logic in that?

Peggy: I'm a woman.

Eamonn: I suppose there ought to be a law . . .

Peggy: Precisely. Anyway, it will hurt me more than it hurts you.

(*Eamonn feels his jaw.*)

Eamonn: I doubt that.

Peggy: It will show that you care about retaining my respect; that you can love somebody else more than yourself — if only for a moment.

Eamonn: A very painful moment.

Peggy: I've a good dentist. Yes or no?

Eamonn: Anything else, Pegtops —

Peggy: I don't want anything else. Yes or no?

Eamonn: (*slowly*) Well, then, no.

(*Peggy turns towards her mother and takes her arm.*)

Peggy: Come on, Mumsie. Let's go home.

(*Delightedly, Chris puts on his jacket.*)

Chris: I may have my faults, but at least I can support you.

Eamonn: You're clever, Father. You foresaw that this was going to happen.

(*Father McMahon smiles, but makes no reply. The whole party moves, left, towards the door leading to the landing and the staircase. Murphy picks up the suitcase. Once Peggy looks back at Eamonn, hoping that even now he will give her a reason to return. Suddenly Eamonn overtakes them in a few strides and plants himself between them and the door.*)

Eamonn: Stop!

Chris: Stop, says our hero.

(*The others pause, but Chris continues to advance. Eamonn puts up his fists.*)

Eamonn: Stop, I tell you.

Chris: You're too late, Sonny Jim. Now move aside, like a good little boy. I don't want you to get hurt.

Eamonn: You're not taking Peggy from here.

(*Chris sweeps Eamonn aside.*)

Chris: Out of my way, I said.

(*Eamonn falls full length. Peggy puts her hand to her face.*)

Mrs Quin: Oh, good heavens! Evie! Evie!

(*Eamonn scrambles to his feet and flings himself on Chris. Chris wrenches himself free, then fells Eamonn with an expertly delivered blow.*)

Mrs Quin: He's been killed!

(*Sir Henry pats her arm soothingly.*)

Sir Henry: Men will be men, you know.

(*Peggy hastens forward and kneels down beside Eamonn, tending him.*)

Sir Henry: (*to Chris*) You've beaten him.
Peggy: (*to Eamonn*) Are you all right, darling?

(*Eamonn groans.*)

Chris: No, damn him, he's beaten me.
Father McMahon: You're right, son. I hadn't foreseen this.
Chris: Come on, Peggy. I hardly touched him.
Peggy: You don't know your own strength, you big brute.
Chris: I tell you, he's shamming. I demand that he be examined by a doctor.
Peggy: I thought you didn't believe in doctors.
Chris: They're good enough if a chap is shamming. They're only no good if he isn't.
Sir Henry: Remember in the Desert Campaign, chap swore he had been wounded in the foot. Only after they'd amputated his leg, they found he hadn't been in action at all that day.
Chris: I'll get a doctor myself.

(*Father McMahon puts a hand on his shoulder.*)

Father McMahon: I'll go, son. I've got to be getting along anyway.
Chris: Right, Father. Thanks. I'll send you that cheque.
Father McMahon: Do.

(*On his way, left, to the outer door, he pauses to examine the small picture on the easel. Sir Henry follows him.*)

Sir Henry: I'm with you, Padre.
Murphy: Why don't you buy it, Father?
Father McMahon: How much?
Murphy: Fifty pounds.
Father McMahon: Is it worth fifty pounds?

(*Sir Henry peers at the picture in passing, twirls his moustache, and waits for the priest by the door.*)

Murphy: If you hung that picture on the wall of your house, it would be the same as having a fifty-pound note pinned up on the wall.

Father McMahon: It seems a little slight for fifty pounds. (*To Peggy.*) Will you take the word of the doctor as to whether (*he nods towards the prone Eamonn*) he's shamming or not?

Mrs Quin: Do as Father McMahon suggests, Peggy.

Father McMahon: You think you can make a good husband out of him, don't you?

Peggy: Yes. Yes, I do.

Father McMahon: It wouldn't be a good start to let him humbug you.

(*Peggy speaks reluctantly, half addressing herself to Eamonn also.*)

Peggy: If the doctor says he's shamming, I'll — I'll go home.

Father McMahon: Good girl!

(*He leaves with the Colonel.*)

Peggy: Help me get him on to the bed.

Chris: (*folding his arms*) Not me.

Mrs Quin: Do lend a hand, Chris dear.

Peggy: (*to Chris, firmly*) Come on. And you too, Mr Murphy.

Murphy: (*to Chris*) Come on, man. (*He puts down the suitcase.*) She'll get her way in the end.

(*He leads the reluctant Chris forward. Mrs Quin suddenly becomes flustered.*)

Mrs Quin: Oh good gracious me, what am I thinking of, standing here. I must get some hot water. Evie! Evie! Oh no, of course, Evie isn't here. I'll ask the landlady downstairs. And some Jeyes Fluid. No, not Jeyes Fluid.

(*She bustles out of the room.*)

Peggy: Thanks, Mother. I'll be with you in a moment.

(*Meanwhile the two men have lifted Eamonn over to the bed. As they deposit him Chris, who carries his legs, throws them down roughly. Peggy crosses to the outer door.*)

Peggy: Look after him properly.

Chris: The precious little lamb won't die.

(*Peggy leaves the room.*)

Chris: (*to Eamonn*) Come on, open your eyes.

(*There is no movement.*)

Chris: You're quite safe now. Your audience has gone.

(*Eamonn slowly opens his eyes, then half raises himself and unconcernedly turns over on his elbow.*)

Chris: Playing on her maternal instincts, eh?

(*Eamonn smiles broadly.*)

Chris: Wait until the doctor comes.

(*He strolls over to the window and gazes out. Murphy produces a small illustrated catalogue from his pocket.*)

Murphy: Nothing like new chair covers and curtains for oiling the wheels of matrimony. Women can't stand a sordid atmosphere, even in a garret. Here are some inexpensive hats —

Eamonn: You sell hats as well?

Murphy: Everything that you need from the cradle to the grave. If Murphy's Mammoth Store were to be excavated in two thousand years time, you would be able to reconstruct the whole life of man as lived under the rule of Fianna Fail.

Chris: The economic ice age.

Murphy: These hats, judiciously produced from time to time, are guaranteed to smooth out all matrimonial differences.

Eamonn: Marriage, if you believe in it, is a pact of mutual esteem between two civilised and rational beings. You can't buy the affection of your wife with hats and chair covers.

Murphy: Ah, there you're mistaken. Until men overcome their sentimental fallacy that women are civilised and rational beings, and recognise that they are attractive savages, with whom one string of coloured glass beads counts for more than half a dozen noble deeds, or half a hundred high-minded sentiments, there can be no future for marriage.

Eamonn: Very well. Let's cut it short. The doctor may be here any minute. What can you let me have for fifty pounds?

Murphy: Say, two hats, two chair covers, and a pair of curtains.

Chris: I'd like to see Peggy wearing anything less than a model hat!

(*Eamonn, ignoring Chris, speaks to Murphy. He points to the small picture on the easel.*)

Eamonn: There's your fifty pound note.
Murphy: You're going to pay me with that — daub!
Eamonn: Good as a fifty pound note, you said. And to Father McMahon. You wouldn't lie to a priest, would you, Mr Murphy?
Murphy: Well, you little . . . Well . . .
Eamonn: Would you, Mr Murphy?
Murphy: If I told Father McMahon — if I told him that picture was worth fifty pounds, then it is worth fifty pounds.

(*He glares at Eamonn.*)

Eamonn: Precisely, Mr Murphy. And in return for my making over to you this picture which is as good as a fifty pound note, you will deliver the goods as promised to this address. Isn't that so, Mr Murphy?

(*Murphy swallows hard.*)

Eamonn: Isn't that so, Mr Murphy?
Murphy: (*faintly*) Yes.
Eamonn: Here's your catalogue.

(*Murphy snatches it from him and stuffs it into his pocket.*)

Murphy: I must be going now.
Eamonn: You can take the picture with you.

(*The Indian ornament on the table catches Murphy's eye. At once he becomes more cheerful.*)

Murphy: Right!
Eamonn: Glad you're being more pleasant about it.

(*Murphy picks up the ornament and examines it.*)

Murphy: Worth fifty pounds, you said. Fits into my pocket, see? You don't mind, do you?

(*He makes for the outer door.*)

Eamonn: Thief! Dirty thief! Have you no respect for other people's property?

(*He swings himself off the bed and follows Murphy. The latter, in his haste to escape, almost collides with Sir Henry, Father McMahon and Dr O'Donovan, who stand at the door.)*

Murphy: Excuse me, Father. Sir Henry.
Father McMahon: What's the matter? This is the doctor.
Eamonn: The doctor? Oh, the doctor!

(He hastens back to the bed, this time making sure that he has a limp. Murphy seizes the chance to slip out. Chris comes forward eagerly from the window.)

Chris: Ah, now we shall see!
Sir Henry: Think I ought to fetch the ladies.
Chris: Do, Sir Henry. I'd like to have Peggy here when this — this fellow is shown up.

(Sir Henry goes out.)

Father McMahon: Gentlemen, this is Dr O'Donovan. Doctor, here is your patient.

(Dr O'Donovan approaches Eamonn. He speaks in his brightest bedside manner.)

Dr O'Donavan: And now, what seems to be the trouble?
Eamonn: Excuse me, Doctor — I ask merely on a point of information — why do you doctors always say: And now, what seems to be the trouble?
Dr O'Donovan: It's quite simple. If you say: what is the trouble?, then you risk frightening the patient by suggesting that there is necessarily something wrong with him. On the other hand, if you syggest that there is nothing wrong with him, then you risk giving him the idea that your services are superfluous.
Eamonn: I see.
Dr O'Donavan: What is wanted is a nice ambiguity. It leaves the patient comfortable, without imperilling that gratitude on his part which is such an asset when charging high fees.
Eamonn: You've a right to gratitude when you cure a man.
Dr O'Donavan: Good heavens, we never cure anyone.
Chris: What!
Dr O'Donovan: No, no, no. That's no part of the function of the medical profession. For instance, when a politician finds himself opposed by a force which he cannot control, he at once places

himself at the head of it, thus giving the electorate the impression that he is leading it. So when he is called upon to make drastic cuts in public expenditure, but knows that the voters will have none of it, he informs them that such cuts are totally unnecessary. Wisely he sees that he cannot possibly bankrupt the country, since the country is bankrupt already.

Chris: What about the Leader of the Opposition?

Dr O'Donovan: The Leader of the Opposition thinks, tells the truth, and tries to do something — a fatal combination in Irish politics.

Eamonn: So a doctor avoids doing anything but simply places himself at the head of whatever is going to happen anyway?

Dr O'Donovan: Precisely. Knowing that he cannot cure his patient — he concentrates on making sure that he himself has at least one good suit, a fund of anecdotes to ingratiate himself with the patient's relatives, and an enigmatic smile. Then, if the patient recovers, people say: He knew all along that all would be well. If he dies, they say: He knew that the case was hopeless, but wanted to keep up our spirits.

Eamonn: So a doctor has nothing to learn?

Dr O'Donovan: (*sharply*) I never said that. He must learn to play golf really well, to keep his hands off the nurses, and to make himself a master of inactivity. (*He bends over the bed.*) And now, as I said before, what seems to be the trouble?

Eamonn: The trouble seems to be in my right leg.

Chris: The trouble for him is that there isn't any trouble.

(*At this moment Sir Henry returns with Peggy and Mrs Quin.*)

Peggy: The landlady was out. How is he, Doctor?

Dr O'Donovan: (*manipulating the leg*) Does that hurt?

Eamonn: (*cautiously*) Should it?

Dr O'Donovan: Well, yes, if you've given it a strain.

Eamonn: Then it hurts.

O'Donavan: He may well have given it a bit of a strain.

Chris: But nothing of any moment? In fact, hardly anything at all?

Dr O'Donovan: Perhaps so.

Chris: (*to Peggy*) You have heard the expert opinion of a first- rate medical man.

Dr O'Donovan: On the other hand, it would be better for him to lie up for a bit.

Eamonn: (*to Peggy*) One doesn't, you know, have to lie up for nothing.

Chris: I always knew that doctors were useless.

Dr O'Donovan: (*glancing at his watch*) I've a call to make. A very involved case — squint, complicated by a twisted bowel.

Father McMahon: I think we all ought to be going.

(*There is a general movement towards the outer door.*)

Mrs Quin: Peggy, aren't you coming?

Peggy: I'm staying to nurse Eamonn.

Chris: He doesn't need any nursing.

Peggy: Don't worry, Mother. I'll sleep in the annex. (*She points to the door in the right-hand wall.*) We'll get married as soon as Eamonn has recovered. Won't we, Eamonn?

(*He makes no reply.*)

Peggy: Won't we, Eamonn?

Eamonn: Well, if you must know — as a matter of fact . . .

Peggy: As a matter of fact what?

Eamonn: It's against my principles. Marriage, I mean.

Father McMahon: This is really too bad!

(*Peggy opens her bag, takes out her cigarette case, and lights up a cigarette.*)

Sir Henry: Should be stood up against a wall!

Mrs Quin: Didn't you promise to marry her?

Eamonn: Had to, you see, to get her to come away with me. Once away, I knew I'd be able to talk sense into her.

(*Chris has begun to drift towards the window, and Peggy towards her mother.*)

Mrs Quin: So my daughter isn't good enough to be your wife! Chris, have you heard all this?

(*Chris appears to be absorbed by the street below, and doesn't answer.*)

Mrs Quin: Chris, are you expecting someone?

Chris: No. No.

(*He leaves the window, but then drifts back to it again. Meanwhile Peggy has reached her mother and whispers something to her.*)

Mrs Quin: I've a surprise for you all. Peggy has decided to stay on with Eamonn.

Peggy: I've taken on a job, Father, and I think I ought to see it through.

(*She crosses to Eamonn, who catches hold of her hand.*)

Eamonn: I knew you'd understand, darling.

Father McMahon: What's this?

(*Eamonn takes the cigarette case which Peggy still holds in her hand, and examines it. While he does so, she goes to Father McMahon and murmurs something to him.*)

Eamonn: Moorish! The cigarette case I gave you!

Father McMahon: (*to Peggy*) Very well.

(*Peggy returns to Eamonn to retrieve her cigarette case.*)

Father McMahon: As for you, young man, all I can say is: God help you. From now on, you are going to have a fight on your hands, compared with which your little difference with Chris is going to seem like nothing at all.

Eamonn: A fight I propose to win.

Father McMahon: You'll have to support her. (*He turns to the large painting on the wall.*) That picture of yours of the Crucifixion — how much is it?

Eamonn: Er — um — well, I suppose —

Peggy: (*decisively*) Sixty pounds.

Father McMahon: (*taken aback*) Sixty! You wouldn't think thirty . . .

Peggy: Sixty. We can't let it go for a penny less.

Father McMahon: (*to Eamonn*) You see what I mean! (*He considers.*) I'll take it for my church.

Sir Henry: Buying a Crucifixion painted by an impious atheist!

Father McMahon: No one is outside the glory of God. Besides, why should the Devil have all the best pictures, and God be fobbed off with the mass-produced monstrosities that make hideous so many Irish homes?

Sir Henry: But an artist who treats of an occasion for which he has no reverence! Peel potatoes, I say.

Eamonn: I have reverence. I have reverence for a great and beautiful story. I have reverence for the integrity of my own work.

(*Sir Henry throws up his hands in bewilderment.*)

Father McMahon: Come, Doctor, I've kept you waiting too long. You have a difficult case.

Dr O'Donovan: In addition to squint and a twisted bowel, there may be a floating kidney.

(*He goes out. Father McMahon follows him, pausing to take down the picture. He turns to Eamonn.*)

Father McMahon: You'll find a cheque for fifty-eight pounds in the post tomorrow.

Eamonn: Sixty.

Father McMahon: I'm taking two pounds for my missionary box.

(*Eamonn sits up in the bed and shouts after him.*)

Eamonn: Bare-faced highway robbery!

Father McMahon: It is. But the highway leads to God.

(*He leaves. Peggy pushes Eamonn down. She speaks to the others.*)

Peggy: Now off with you! I must attend to my patient.

(*Chris in consternation glances at his watch, then cranes out of the window and looks up and down the street.*)

Sir Henry: Come on, man! Don't you know when parade has been dismissed?

(*Chris, after a final glance out of the window, follows them towards the outer door. As they approach it, a commotion is heard on the staircase, and Norah's voice calls out.*)

Norah: Mrs Quin! M'am!
Chris: Who's that?
Mrs Quin: It's — it's Norah.

(*Chris smiles to himself. Norah enters, very much out of breath.*)

Norah: Excuse me, m'am — till I get me breath. Them stairs is steep.

(*She glances at Chris.*)

Mrs Quin: Has anything happened, Norah?

(*Norah hesitates. Chris encourages her with a glance and a nod. Norah points at Eamonn.*)

Norah: It's him. He run out on me. He promised to marry me.

(*Eamonn sits up sharply.*)

Eamonn: What!

Norah: He said he'd marry me. (*To Eamonn.*) Thought you could run out on me, did you?

Peggy: Eamonn, is this true?

Eamonn: Of course not.

(*Norah thrusts her left hand forward for Peggy's inspection.*)

Norah: Look what he gave me.

Peggy: It's an engagement ring! It — it looks oriental. Colonel, you've served in India. What d'you make of it?

(*Sir Henry advances. Norah thrusts out her hand.*)

Sir Henry: Not Indian. Should say it's — Moorish.

Peggy: Moorish! Thank you, Sir Henry. (*To Eamonn*) You seem to buy your presents wholesale.

Eamonn: Look here, Peggy . . . Norah, what is all this?

Sir Henry: Always said the fellow was a bounder — a Moorish bounder.

Mrs Quin: An African cad.

Peggy: Mother, would you help me to pack. I've my shoulder bag in the annex.

Mrs Quin: Certainly. He can't treat my daughter like a (*an icy glance at Eamonn*) houri.

(*They have just reached the inner door, when Norah staggers and almost falls.*)

Eamonn: Look out!

Chris: She's all right.

Mrs Quin: What's the matter, Norah?

Norah: Just — I come up the stairs too quick.

Chris: Just give her time to get her breath back.

(*Eamonn gets off the bed. He limps across to Norah dragging a chair with him.*)

Eamonn: What's wrong with you people? Can't you see the girl's ill!
Peggy: Ought we to get the doctor back?
Eamonn: Sit down, Norah.

(*She does so, and puts her head in her right hand. He remains standing by her, supporting himself by the back of the chair.*)

Chris: Nonsense! You don't want the doctor, do you, Norah?

(*Sir Henry wheels round and makes for the outer door.*)

Chris: (*alarmed*) Where are you going, Colonel?
Sir Henry: Fetch doctor.
Chris: I'll go.
Sir Henry: Very well.
Chris: Don't suppose I'll be able to find him.

(*He goes out.*)

Mrs Quin: Come, Peggy, let's pack. Illness must not prevent us from doing our moral duty.
Eamonn: Moral duty? Packing?
Mrs Quin: (*stiffly*) There can be great moral beauty in the correct packing of a shoulder-bag.

(*Peggy and she disappear into the annex. Sir Henry exhibits discomfort at finding himself alone with the miscreants.*)

Sir Henry: I'll — I'll just dodge outside to smoke a pipe.

(*He leaves by the outer door.*)

Eamonn: Chris put you up to this, didn't he?

(*Norah makes no reply. He takes her left hand.*)

Eamonn: I suppose he gave you this ring. Moorish, eh? Fellow's got subtlety.

(*He lets go her hand. She lifts up her head from her other hand.*)

Norah: I'm sorry, Mr Eamonn. I had to —

(*She is interrupted by Chris's bursting into the room.*)

Chris: Ah, she is better. Mrs Quin! Peggy!
Mrs Quin: Yes dear?

(*She enters, followed by Peggy.*)

Chris: Couldn't find the doctor anywhere.

Eamonn: You can't have done more than glance up and down the street.

Chris: I *gazed* up and down the street.

(*Peggy gives an unhappy glance towards Eamonn.*)

Peggy: Well, I suppose I'd better finish my packing.

Chris: Do, darling. I got the taxi to wait. I'll tell the driver.

(*He leaves and can be heard descending the staircase.*)

Mrs Quin: (*to Peggy*) I'll go on, dear. I find the stairs a little trying.

(*She follows Chris. Peggy turns towards the annex.*)

Eamonn: Peggy!

Peggy: Well?

Eamonn: One minute. Norah, Peggy and I love one another. You know what that means. Norah, this is my last chance.

Norah: (*doggedly*) You promised to marry me.

(*Peggy shrugs and turns to go. As she does so, there is a tap on the outer door. She pauses.*)

Peggy: Come in.

(*Dr O'Donovan enters.*)

Dr O'Donovan: Excuse me. I think I left my stethoscope behind.

Eamonn: Did you meet Mrs Quin?

Dr O'Donovan: I met no one. I just popped in to see a patient downstairs. He has been in much pain.

Peggy: I hope he is more comfortable now.

Dr O'Donovan: Much. He is dead. And now, my stethoscope.

(*Peggy indicates Norah.*)

Peggy: This girl has been very unwell.

(*Dr O'Donovan crosses to Norah. Eamonn makes room for him by limping back to the bed, on which he sits.*)

Dr O'Donovan: Ah, indeed! Well, my dear, what seems to be the trouble?

Norah: I was sort of dizzy — and sick.

Dr O'Donovan: Always masticate well. You may have bitten off more than you could chew. Open your mouth. Stick out your tongue.

(*Dr O'Donovan passes his hands over her body.*)

Eamonn: What are you keeping so dark, Dr O'Donovan?
Dr O'Donovan: Nothing that won't see the light of day.
Peggy: What puzzles me, Eamonn, is: if it's against your principles to marry me, why isn't it against them to marry Norah?
Eamonn: And that's what puzzles me too, Peggy.

(*Sir Henry enters.*)

Sir Henry: Just dodged out to smoke a pipe.
Dr O'Donovan: The girl's going to have a baby.
Sir Henry: Impossible!
Dr O'Donovan: It's been done before.
Sir Henry: This would never have happened under Winston Churchill.

(*Peggy crosses to Eamonn.*)

Peggy: Why — why Eamonn, it couldn't have been . . .
Eamonn: So that's why the poor girl was in such a hurry to find a husband!

(*Peggy sits down on the bed beside him and links her arm through his.*)

Peggy: I wonder if I'm destined to spend my life apologising to you.)
Eamonn: And getting me knocked down by your tame Strong Man.
Peggy: I think it's you that are The Strong Man.
Sir Henry: Who can be the father?

(*Dr O'Donovan picks up his stethoscope off the end of the bed. He crosses to the outside door.*)

Dr O'Donovan: That's outside my province. I can only find the child.

(*Sir Henry shakes his head gravely.*)

Sir Henry: Must write a letter to the 'Irish Times'. Don't know what the editor will think.

(*Dr O'Donovan goes out.*)

Norah: Mr Chris is the father.
Eamonn: Always thought he had a good first service.

Sir Henry: Seems to have made a double fault!

Peggy: Poor Mother!

Norah: Don't tell the mistress, Miss Peggy. Me Da still has a job to lose.

Peggy: Mother mustn't be told, Sir Henry. Chris was almost her son.

(*Sir Henry turns to Norah.*)

Sir Henry: We'll see that you get restitution from the proper quarter.

(*Mrs Quin enters from the outer door. Peggy hurriedly rises and moves away from Eamonn.*)

Mrs Quin: Why didn't you follow me, Peggy?

Peggy: Sir Henry and I will be with you in a minute.

Mrs Quin: Chris is waiting in the taxi.

(*Peggy crosses to the annex.*)

Peggy: I'll finish my packing.

(*Mrs Quin follows her.*)

Mrs Quin: I see I shall have to help you, dear, if we're ever to get away.

(*Chris enters.*)

Chris: What's keeping everyone?

Mrs Quin: I'll have them down to the taxi in three minutes.

Chris: Good. The sooner we part company with this gentleman (*he indicates Eamonn*), the cleaner I, personally, shall feel.

Mrs Quin: I cannot but agree with you.

(*Chris crosses to Peggy. He is enormously pleased with himself.*)

Chris: Well, darling, I think you now know the difference between that fellow and me.

(*He puts his arm round her waist.*)

Peggy: I most certainly do.

Chris: promise never to have any doubts about me again.

Peggy: With all my heart.

(*Chris crosses to Sir Henry.*)

Chris: Well, Colonel, you wanted to solve this little triangle by sending us both off to be butchered. (*He claps him on the back.*) You wouldn't want to send us now.

Sir Henry: Not both.

Chris: So you see, there's something in class distinction after all.

Eamonn: (*facetiously*) First class, second class and third class.

Mrs Quin: (*frostily*) I don't care to joke about sacred matters. Peggy, let's go and pack.

Peggy: Certainly, Mother.

Chris: Physical culture makes a man's character as straight as it makes his limbs.

Eamonn: In that case you must have rickets.

(*Peggy and Mrs Quin go into the annex. Chris speaks with superb finality.*)

Chris: I can afford to ignore that. The whole subject is closed.

(*Mrs Quin safely out of the way, the storm bursts upon him.*)

Eamonn: Oh no, it's not.

Sir Henry: Only just beginning, m' lad.

Eamonn: You thundering great hypocrite!

Sir Henry: Ought to be horsewhipped!

Chris: What — what's happened, Colonel?

Sir Henry: Cat's out of the bag. That's what's happened.

Norah: Mr Chris, the doctor was here.

Chris: God! Did — did he find out what was wrong?

Sir Henry: Yes, sir, he did. And it wasn't housemaid's knee.

Chris: And everyone was in the room when I came in! Everyone has heard! I'm ruined, ruined!

(*Mrs Quin comes out hurriedly from the annex.*)

Mrs Quin: What's happened?

(*Chris strides over to her.*)

Chris: What can you have been thinking of me?

(*Sir Henry clears his throat loudly. Eamonn gesticulates in an attempt to attract Chris's attention.*)

Chris: I know how strict you are. And for her and me to have a baby this way! Out of wedlock!

(*Mrs Quin glances towards the annex, supposing that he is talking about Peggy.*)

Mrs Quin: And the child never breathed a word of it to me!

Chris: And to have the news come out on the very eve of the wedding!

Mrs Quin: Nonsense, dear Chris! What's the real harm!

Chris: What!

(*She kisses him on the cheek.*)

Mrs Quin: Dear, Peggy and you would have had babies anyway. What does an extra one matter?

(*Chris starts back in amazement.*)

Sir Henry: Er — Chris — er, some things are — er — not what they seem.

Chris: What's that?

Sir Henry: Er — some people don't know as much as — other people know.

Chris: Well, I know that.

Sir Henry: And other people have a greater knowledge of the facts than — some people have.

Chris: You don't say!

Mrs Quin: The Colonel means, the facts of life.

(*Sir Henry pulls at his moustache in embarrassment, walks away, and looks out of the window.*)

Chris: Oh. (*To Mrs Quin*) I suppose I shall have to marry her now.

Mrs Quin: (*sharply*) What d'you mean?

Chris: Well, how can I get out of it?

Mrs Quin: Don't you want to marry her?

Chris: Her family is hardly up to mine.

Mrs Quin: Really!

Chris: Fancy having an illiterate old harridan for a mother-in-law!

(*Norah starts angrily.*)

Mrs Quin: Thank you! Thank you very much!

  (*She walks furiously to the annex.*) Peggy! Peggy!

(*There is the sound of rapid footsteps ascending the staircase, and Murphy bursts into the room. He makes straight for Nora.*)

Murphy: You poor child! I met the doctor. I learnt everything.

(*He takes her hand and pumps her arm up and down in sympathy. Sir Henry and Eamonn exchange glances of consternation.*)

Murphy: Whoever the man is who is the father of your baby, I'd never agree to do business with him, I don't care who he is.

Nora: Thank you, sir.

Murphy: And if ever I found that I had taken money from him, I'd fling it back in his face.

Eamonn: You may be letting yourself in for an expensive time, Murphy.

(*Murphy pulls a catalogue out of his pocket which he shows to Nora.*)

Murphy: Now we must be practical, my dear. Here we have some most inexpensive layettes.

(*Mrs Quin, who has paused at the door to the annex, has been looking back and forth between Nora and Chris with a puzzled expression.*)

Mrs Quin: Nora, what is all this?

Murphy: Layettes in both colours. Here we have the Murphy Symphony in Blue for Bouncing Boys —

Mrs Quin: (*to Nora*) Am I to understand that an irregularity has taken place?

Murphy: — and a Fantasia in close fitting flannelette of Pixie Pink for Female Infants.

Mrs Quin: Chris! Nora! I see it all!

(*Murphy turns to Mrs Quin in consternation.*)

Murphy: It's Chris, is it! Oh, well . . . Quite romantic if you think about it, m'am. The prince and the beggar girl.

Mrs Quin: Chris, how could you so have forgotten your station?

Murphy: Nature is always democratic, m'am.

Mrs Quin: Mr Murphy, kindly do not mention nature to me. I refuse to wallow in licentious subjects.

(*Peggy enters wearing her shoulder bag.*)

Peggy: Well, Mother, I'm packed. Off we go!

Eamonn: Peggy, you're not going now!

Peggy: *(frigidly)* Naturally, Mr O'Sullivan. *(She takes Chris's arm.)* Come along, darling.

Chris: After — after my behaviour!

Peggy: So Mother knows! We were trying to spare your feelings, Mother.

(She disengages herself from Chris and crosses to Eamonn.)

Eamonn: So little Pegtops is coming to live with me after all!

Mrs Quin: I had already sent for Evie. She'll be here directly. She will remain as chaperon.

(Eamonn turns to Peggy.)

Eamonn: We are to live together —

Peggy: — as nurse and patient.

Eamonn: This — this is blackmail!

Peggy: It is.

(Mrs Quin turns towards Chris.)

Mrs Quin: You, I take it, have already proposed to Norah?

Chris: No.

Mrs Quin: Kindly do so, in my hearing.

(Reluctantly, Chris addresses himself to Norah. His tone is sulky.)

Chris: Will you marry me?

(Norah is across to him in a flash and takes his arm.)

Norah: May we live in Phibsboro'?

Mrs Quin: Certainly not. There are limits to a man's degradation.

Eamonn: Peggy, I give in. I'll marry you.

Peggy: Darling!

Eamonn: I never thought I'd stoop to such immorality. But a chaperon!

Peggy: I told Mother that would finish you. *(She kisses him.)* My Strong Man!

Eamonn: I think you're the strongest of us all.

(Sir Henry, who has been continuing to look out of the window, suddenly speaks.)

Sir Henry: Another taxi has just drawn up. It's — yes, it's Evie!

Mrs Quin: Evie! Let me see.

(She hurries over to the window.)

Sir Henry: By Jove! What a figure!

Mrs Quin: The shameless hussy! She's practically only wearing a bikini.

Sir Henry: Weather's very sultry. The poor girl's only trying to keep herself cool.

(*Norah has joined them at the window.*)

Norah: 'Tis shameless she is! Nearly topless.

(*Chris, who has followed Norah, also looks out.*)

Chris: That shows you what physical culture can do. Just look at those fabulous legs!

(*Peggy has now joined them.*)

Peggy: She'll not come up here dressed like that!

(*Eamonn is craning over her shoulder.*)

Eamonn: What a model she'd make! Look at those hips!

Mrs Quin: She's coming up the stairs. Now everybody back quickly. We must give her a warm welcome. I'll speak to her later about her costume.

(*They all hasten to cluster near the outer door. Murphy pulls a garment out of his pocket and displays it.*)

Murphy: I'll show her the Murphy Modulated Mini-panties for the Modern Miss.

(*Mrs Quin advances towards the door with her right hand extended.*)

Mrs Quin: Evie! Evie! Delighted to see you, Evie!

But, before Evie can appear,

THE CURTAIN FALLS

CRITIQUES

'TWELFTH NIGHT'
(GATE THEATRE, DUBLIN)

He's an over-rated fellow, this Shakespeare. If he were merely esteemed as the greatest dramatist of his day, I should have no quarrel with him. It is plain that his dramatic output as far outweighs that of any of his coevals as, before him, Chaucer's output of narrative verse outweighed that of any of his. Even if the claim were to be raised one place higher, and he was held to be the greatest writer, dramatist or otherwise, of his time, that is a position that might be maintained, for Spenser was before him, and Milton after. But this solitary pinnacle upon which he is placed, this monstrous and inflated prestige, this runaway reputation, this gigantic blown-up balloon, this infliction upon schoolboys, this divinity, this man whose most inconsiderable dramatic pieces are revived in reverence, this literacy monster to whom we go in the theatre, cap in hand, not to praise nor to blame, but to absorb as one absorbs gospel! The very act of writing disparagingly of him has become more than an act of criticism. It has become an act of courage.

How was it sown, this fantastic mushroom of his reputation, and how grew it? Like all very large institutions, it was sown upon a soil of real achievement, and forced in the hot-house of repetition, of many voices averring that its size and quality were such and such, and more voices catching up the phrases and reverberating the cant from one generation to another, until it became a heresy to deny it. It is the technique of advertisement, of propaganda, of ballyhoo. Repeat a thing often enough, long enough and loud enough, and behold, it is dogma, an institution. There is only one mustard — Coleman's mustard. If you have fleas, you do not look beyond

Keatings. Guinness is good for you. Bob Martins will put your dog, any dog, half a dozen dogs, right. 'Shakespeare is not our poet, but the world's' (including Eire and the Six Counties).

Grimly Dissatisfied Interpolator: When you've finished this schoolboy outburst, try and tell us what exactly you think you're getting at.

Dorman: Talking of schoolboys, I remember as a schoolboy seeing Mrs Patrick Campbell and Agnew McMaster playing at the Abbey Theatre in a season of Shakespeare and Ibsen. At the beginning of the week I saw them playing in *Macbeth*, and at the end in *Ghosts*. And what a clumsy bungler, what an amateur of the theatre, did not Ibsen make Shakespeare look.

Grimly Dissatisfied Interpolator: *Macbeth* is not one of Shakespeare's best plays, I mean, as a stage piece. It has magnificent flashes of poetry, it has at least one great character, it is splendid to read, but it lacks tautness; it sprawls. Now take *Othello*, or *Coriolanus*! Also, Shakespeare's plays were not conceived in terms of our stage. That gives Ibsen the advantage.

Dorman: Shall I ever forget *Coriolanus* at the Abbey Theatre some years ago! Such rant! It surpassed Dryden and Corneille. Everybody on the stahe spent the evening waving his arms and shouting. The Gordon Riots weren't in it. The English guest actor who played Coriolanus had the lungs of a lion. I still recall with horror his pale feverish face, and the great ever-open circle of his mouth in the midst of it, pouring out a merciless cascade of din on the quivering audience. As to your second point, the modern theatre can be made amply simple and fluid to stage Elizabethan plays, as Mr John Izon has recently shown us in his admirable and swift-moving productions of *Romeo and Juliet* and *Twelfth Night* for Lord Longford's company at the Gate Theatre. However, let us grant that Shakespeare, on the strength of *Othello* and *Hamlet*, is one of the greatest tragedians of the world.

GDI: Then you admit you've been talking nonsense?

Dorman: Not at all. Consider him as a comedian. Take *Twelfth Night*, for instance. Was there ever a lamer, a more naive, plot? A chit of a girl is shipwrecked on the coast of Illyria, a country which is to her foreign soil. From the captain of the wrecked vessel she enquires the name of its ruler. On learning that it is the duke Orsino, she gets the somewhat tortuous notion into her pretty head of disguising her sex and serving the duke as his eunuch. The job falls into her lap (were there no better qualified eunuchs in Illyria?). And so on through the play. People enter and exit, and fall in and out of love, precisely when the intricacies of the plot demand, and without the slightest regard to the probabilities either of external events or human psychology.

'Ah,' but says the university don, holding up a finger and smiling roguishly, as if excusing the naughtiness of a favourite pupil, 'Shakespeare himself felt all this. Does he not make Fabian say, albeit in a restricted context, "If this were played upon a stage now, I could condemn it as an improbable fiction"? Is not the very sub-title he has given the play, "What You Will", that is, belonging to no particular dramatic genre?'

And that, apparently, makes it all right.

Much of the dialogue is equally naive. Consider Sir Andrew's remark to Maria: 'Fair lady, do you think you have fools in hand?', and the obvious, clumsy, schoolgirl retort, 'Sir, I have not you by the hand.' While on the subject of fools, was there ever a drearier set of stage characters than the professional fools of Shakespeare's plays, with their inevitable quips about the wit of fools and the folly of wits, their smart verbal snip-snap à la John Lyly, and their endless babu philosophisings. The disease of punning extends from the Fools to all the other comic characters.

Sir Toby: Taste your legs sir, put them to motion.

Viola: My legs do better understand me, sir, when I understand what you mean by bidding me taste my legs.

Sir Toby: I mean, to go, sir, to enter.

Viola: I will answer you with gait and entrance.

Grimly Dissatisfied Interpolator: It is easy to pick holes in a great canvas.

Dorman: An I pick holes in the canvas, sir, the canvas can be no longer wholly great, being diminished by the extent of the greatness of the holes I have picked in it.

GDI: I'faith, the man is not whole in the head. He grates on my nerves.

Dorman: That there are certain scenes of real robust humour and certain situations of true comedy in *Twelfth Night* cannot be denied. Such are the drinking scene between Sir Toby, Sir Andrew, Maria, Feste the clown, and Malvolio; Malvolio's finding of the letter, purporting to come from the countess Olivia, but in reality forged by Maria and purposely left in his way; and the duel scene between Sir Andrew, Viola, Sir Toby and Fabian. But when Shakespeare gets hold of a genuinely amusing situation, he proceeds so to labour it, to stretch it out beyond the point which it will bear, and to bury it beneath a mountain of over-preparation, that the little pearl of humour he has placed on the tongue crumbles into powder.

Consider where Malvolio finds the forged letter (not precisely forged, but so we may call it for convenience). Malvolio enters, mincing, attitudinising (for he has an excellent opinion of himself), yet withal grave and soberly clad, with plain black stockings. Maria has already thrown the idea into his head that his mistress Olivia has more than a liking for him. The letter appears to confirm this and, further, enjoins him, if he would please his mistress, to wear yellow stockings cross-gartered and to smile upon every occasion, for 'thy smiles become thee well'. This episode, backed up as it is by the pungent comments of Sir Toby, Sir Andrew, and Fabian hidden in the background, is very funny. Upon Malvolio's exit to make the required changes in his clothing and demeanour, Maria enters, receives the congratulations of the others upon the success of her stratagem, and informs them that her mistress Olivia in fact cannot abide yellow stockings, detests the fashion of cross-gartering, and in her present melancholy state will be in no mood for the smiles of Malvolio.

The audience is now agog to see the outcome when Olivia and Malvolio are brought together. Every morsel of information necessary to the savouring of that situation when it occurs has been fed to them; it is necessary to add nothing more. What does Shakespeare do! Instead of either giving us the scene forthwith or, by some device, screwing it up to some new height of humorous tension, he proceeds methodically to puncture it by over-explanation. First we are given a short scene between Sir Toby, Sir Andrew, and Maria, in which the latter proceeds to describe to the two gentlemen, and to the audience, how Malvolio has already made the changes in his clothing and demeanour precisely according to the letter, and how funny he looks as a consequence. Thus is a part of the situation given to us tamely at second hand, instead of being sprung upon us in its entirety at first. The scene does nothing to heighten the audience's tension and curiosity to see the outcome, for it has merely had the effect of reiterating what everybody already knows.

After a further scene, Olivia and Maria appear, and the former asks for Malvolio. The audience, in spite of all, is already laughing in anticipation, and this laughter is increased when Olivia remarks, 'He (Malvolio) is sad and civil, and suits well for a servant with my fortunes.' If further delay there must be before the protagonists are brought face to face, then a case might be made for Olivia's underlining in another phrase or two the soberness of her own mood and that which she has come to expect from Malvolio. Shakespeare, in fact, does not do this. Instead, he all but succeeds in letting the last bit of wind out of what was, and indeed, despite his best endeavours, still remains a good situation, by making Maria partly prepare her mistress for the change wrought in Malvolio (and thereby prime the audience for the third time).

Grimly Dissatisfied Interpolator: You are judging this play in absolute terms. What of historical perspective? The drama was then still near its infancy. Technique advances; discoveries are made. Therefore an artist must be judged against the background of his own time. Otherwise it would be tantamount to saying that there is more genius in modern art than in the art of bygone days. But genius is genius; a mighty spirit may manifest itself at any time; there is no progression in essential inspiration. I put it to you: Shakespeare wrote the best lyrics. What of the charming romantic element? Did you not pass a pleasant evening at the Gate Theatre?

Dorman: Certainly I passed a pleasant evening. The romantic story was agreeable, if incredible. The comedy was at times very amusing. But 'pleasant;, 'agreeable', 'amusing' — these are not very energetic adjectives of approval. I can find much more forceful words for the cast. Ronald Ibbs extracted every ounce of fun out of Malvolio (what a fine and versatile actor he has become!). Moya Devlin was lovely, dignified and gracious as the countess Olivia. Michael Ripper spoke his lines beautifully, as he always does, but somewhat lacked the presence to sustain the character of the duke Orsino. Wilfrid

Brambell was very funny as Sir Andrew, and Nora O'Mahony, as Maria, gave the lively and polished performance one has come to expect from her. Christopher Casson had to play Feste, the clown, but he sang the exquisite lyrics entrancingly. I have spoken already of the economy of method which John Izon brought to the production, and in this he was well supported with an excellent stage set by Carl Bonn, which allowed of rapid scene changing. These are for me the leading memories of the evening. As for setting Shakespeare's work against the background of his own times, when I think of robust humour or of lyrics, I think of Dekker; when of characters, then Ben Jonson —

GDI: What of Falstaff?

Dorman: Yes, Falstaff was the greatest humorous character of his day, and Shakespeare the best humorist —

GDI: Or of any day.

Dorman: Not by a hundred miles.

GDI: You are probably no critic, sir. You are certainly no gentleman. I shall leave you, sir. I shall mount my bus for Lower Baggot Street, where, thank God, culture is still to be found.

'THE OLD LADY SAYS "NO"'
(GAIETY THEATRE, DUBLIN)

When 'The Old Lady Says "No"' first hit Dublin back in 1929, it hit it with something of the force of a cyclone. Three factors contributed to this effect: the expressionist method of the play, its scarcely veiled allusions to contemporary people and events, and its short way with the sentimental jingoism that ruled the national roost, and perhaps rules it still.

Expressionism was not a new dramatic manner — it had been known earlier in Germany and elsewhere — but it was new to Dublin. Indeed it still remains a novelty to many Dublin playgoers. This I judge from the expressions of bewilderment overheard from many members of the audiences, after the performances at the Gaiety Theatre. It is a drawback of the method, as exemplified in 'The Old Lady', that it overloads the spectator's mind with artistic conventions. First, we have to remember that the speaker is not Robert Emmet, but an actor playing the role of Emmet. True, the author reminds us of the fact from time to time, and Michael MacLiammoir supports him by investing his playing of the part with a marionette- like exaggeration — the exaggeration of a creature pulled, willy-nilly, by strings. But the mind can be an obstinate, or at least forgetful, instrument. It tends to cling to the notion that the gesticulating figure before it is Robert Emmet indeed. Secondly, we are called on to remember that the events unfolding before us take place, not in fact, but in the mind of this Robert Emmet who is not Robert Emmet. Here Hilton Edwards and MacLiammoir assist us by dressing their figures throughout in neutral toned costumes, suggestive of phantoms flitting half glimpsed through the groves and shadows of the mind.

As to the contemporary allusions, these may have lost something of their original sting, but perhaps less so in Ireland than elsewhere, for we as a people live naturally in the past, and bygone people and policies are often more real to us than present. The author has attempted modernisation by the substitution of references to ARP and the rest of it. But is is often a somewhat cold and mechanical business. Perhaps better to leave well alone. A classic is a classic. An exception must be made in favour of the amusing caricatures of Ernest Blythe, Lord Longford and Hilton Edwards, representing our three great theatrical enterprises, on the sofa in the tea party scene.

The calling for a doctor from the audience at the beginning of the play is a prank that the author might have modified with advantage. The audience is alarmed to no dramatic purpose. With the exception of a few problematic groundlings, who might be supposed to welcome a crude stimulant to their bovine nerves, the spectators are sent running off down an emotional cul-de-sac by being made to suffer an emotion which does not grow naturally out of the play. The good-tempered are merely momentarily nonplussed, and the shorter-tempered are irritated by having been led, not down a cul-de-sac, but up the garden path.

So we come to the strongest and the freshest breeze which this play blew into Irish literature, the breeze that disturbed the thickly accumulated cobwebs of sentimental nationalism. The brief introductory scene between the Speaker (Michael MacLiammoir) and Sarah Curran (Meriel Moore) is built up from fragments filched with a purpose from the verses of Mangan, Ferguson, Moore and the rest of the romantic tribe. Here then is the lamb and, shortly afterwards, Denis Johnston enters to the slaughter with his bright sword of modernity and iconoclasm. What parades, what tub-thumping, what praise of patriots, could maintain their fires against the chilly douche delivered by Grattan's statue (Hilton Edwards), in his apostrophe of them as men 'with neither the ability to work nor the courage to wait', word spinners dying gracefully. There has never been a windbag like a patriot in full spate. Denis deflates him.

Other satire there is too: the snob literary yea-party, the empty-headed amours of the two young things from Phibsboro', the callow philosophies of the 'Trinity medical' and his girl-friend, the Government — Department — Preparatory- Schoolmaster approach of the

Minister for Arts and Crafts to art. This general satire, this notion of the mob which is humanity as a many-headed hydra, conducting its affairs and living out its life in a monstrous aggregation of tag phrases and tag moralities ('two apples a penny', 'a few people of taste', 'tennis at Greystones'), is reinforced in the repetitive and choral passages which are so peculiar to the manner of the play. Repetition, regular recurrence of basic motifs, choral passages, these are the stuff of music, and from music has the author drawn a part of his method.

From the very commencement of the play proper, the rhythmic speaking of the lines by the phantom figures establishes the hypnotic mood, which produces an almost trance-like effect on those acting on the stage. The dialogue builds up in cadences to a series of climaxes. If the author has borrowed from music, the producer has, inevitably, borrowed from ballet, and full use was made of grouping and rhythmic gesture. The scene, where the Speaker shoots a member of the crowd closing in upon him, was strangely moving. It is beautifully written, and was as beautifully produced. Hilton Edwards made fine use of complementary red and green in his lighting of it — colours calling to mind Van Gogh's 'Night Cafe', 'where a man might commit a crime'. Nor was the acting of Michael MacLiammoir any whit behind, and the wild beauty of his anguished cry, 'Sally, I do not understand. Sally.', was the crown and apex of the finest moment in the play.

It cannot be denied that there were arid patches. The recital by the Minister's Daughter, which opened the second part, went on too long. So also did the Speaker's orating and the General's singing together in the tea-party scene. Tedious, too, was the Blind Man at his second appearance. The shadows on the screen were intolerably dull. In fact, the whole end of the play dragged. Some might have found its expressionist manner pretentious, that at times it took a long time to say what a more trenchant style could say as well in a single direct line, that it confuses obscurity with profundity. But Swinburne, in the first verse of his chorus from *Atlanta*, takes eight lines to inform us of the fact that winter is coming. Plainly such poetry is directed not to those who are interested only in facts, but to those who are interested also in the manner of their communication. *The Old Lady Says 'No'* is poetic drama; it has a leisurely gait. It has no desire to be obscure; it is merely novel.

The Speaker is undoubtedly Michael MacLiammoir's part, and very perfectly was it played. His talents for broad gesture were given full scope, and the often lively flashes of poetry that light up the play, of which the concluding invocation, 'Strumpet City in the sunset', is but one example, were spoken with fine modulation and sincerity. No less has Meriel Moore made the Old Lady her role, and her transfiguration from the Sarah Curran of sentiment to the Old Flower Woman was little short of miraculous.

Hilton Edwards, as producer, finely translated the text in terms of the stage. For instance, the stage direction reads, 'Upon a pedestal stands Grattan with arm outstretched. He has the face of Major Sirr.' The producer, relying upon the actor's voice to establish the connection between Grattan's statue and Sirr, placed a brilliantly lighted screen behind the figure upon the pedestal, thus presenting the latter as a mere silhouette, a shape, out of which spoke a voice. This was theatrically most effective, and at the same time sacrificed nothing of the author's point. There was the same deft hand apparent in the smallest detail. The text reads, 'Chorus. "An annual subscription of one guinea admits a member to all productions and to all At Homes."' As presented on the stage, the male voices of the Chorus ceased at the word 'productions', and the sentence was concluded by the female voices alone — an effective and lively touch.

THE PLAYS OF TERESA DEEVY
(ABBEY THEATRE, DUBLIN)

I remember some years ago that most intelligent woman of the theatre, Miss Ria Mooney, remarking to me: 'I think the three notable personalities of the most recent generation of Irish playwrights are Sean O'Casey, Denis Johnston, and Teresa Deevy.' The remark stuck in my head, because of my delight at the inclusion of the name of Teresa Deevy. I had but recently seen her play, *Katie Roche*. Beautifully cast and produced by Lennox Robinson, it was playing to tiny houses in the little private Torch Theatre in Knightsbridge, London, at a time when *George and Margaret, French Without Tears, Design for Living*, and similar flapdoodle, were filling the largest theatres of that capital. I felt indignant to think that one of the noblest pieces that had come out of Ireland in a generation should find so comparatively obscure a performance, when so much triviality was drawing audiences in their thousands. I recall seeing Ibsen's *The Doll's House* at the Duke of York's Theatre a few nights after *Katie Roche*, and experiencing no sense of crescendo or decrescendo, but simply of having passed from one masterpiece to another.

Teresa Deevy, like so many writers of the highest talent, has made her way with such quietness and modesty, that she has crept almost unperceived into the front rank. She began her career as a playwright at the time when the first O'Casey plays were making their appearance at the Abbey Theatre. Her first attempt to the Abbey, a play called *After Tomorrow*, was unsuccessful, but her second brought a typed and unsigned offer of help. This she concluded to be from Lady Gregory, who had a reputation for kindness, but it subsequently turned out to be from Lennox Robinson.

Owing to a long illness, she did not accept the offer. On her recovery, she set to work on *Reapers*, which appeared at the Abbey in 1930. She comes of a Waterford family, and *Reapers*, like all her plays, has its setting in the provincial Ireland she understands so delicately and well. It is in many ways a good play, gently ironical, sincere in its avoidance of heroics and a stock conclusion where no conclusion is possible. Nevertheless it is prentice work in comparison with the later full-length plays, which are altogether more interesting and moving.

But first of all we have to notice an amusing little one-act comedy, *In Search of Valour*, produced at the Abbey Theatre the following year (1931). The heroine, Ellie Irwin, a little servant girl, is notable in being the forerunner of, almost a study for, a whole line of heroines in Teresa Deevy's plays: Min Donovan in *Temporal Powers*, Annie Kinsella in *The King of Spain's Daughter*, and Katie Roche herself. All of them share one thing in common, an intense desire to escape from the humdrum ('Would you have us live as snug as the turnips!' cries Katie Roche). All of them wish to enter into that finer, more dangerous world where great deeds are done by men, and inspired by women. Ellie Irwin, 'sixteen, small and sallow with an air of smouldering fury', lives alone with her elderly prayer-mumbling mistress, for whom she nourishes a vast contempt. 'Spirit I like more than prayer,' she informs her. And so it is with all the best of Miss Deevy's heroines.

Ellie Irwin's mistress lives in dread of a call by Jack the Scalp, a notorious killer said to be in hiding from the police in the neighbourhood. Ellie gleefully plays on her mistress's fears. But her real interest is centred on a Mr and Mrs Glitteron, dashing and glamorous neighbours, whom she has never seen, seeking divorce from one another. Ellie's first disappointment comes when Mrs Glitteron enters the room and is discovered to be a cheap vulgar woman. She still has hopes of Mr Glitteron, a man, she feels certain, with 'a great set to his shoulder'. He too enters the room, a little invalid of an old man, on the point of tears. Ellie is desolated.

At this point Jack the Scalp appears. He orders everyone from the room, and barricades the door, determined to sell his life dearly to the dozen armed police without. Ellie alone remains with him. She has found A Man at last. She will share his board and his bed. Jack the Scalp becomes nervous. He protests that he is A Respectable Man. He has never rested his eyes on a woman before. At length he rushes out into the night, prefering the bullets of the police to the blandishments of Ellie. She sighs, 'Why weren't I born in a brave time!'

An altogether more important work, the three-act *Temporal Powers*, appeared at the Abbey in 1932, after tying for first place in the Abbey Theatre Competition with Paul Farrell's *Things That Are Caesar's*. It is marked by the same realism and sincerity as *Reapers*, but is otherwise a work of altogether greater power and interest. The characterisation generally is more sure and deeply felt. There is that simple yet adequate and perfectly fashioned plot, which allows Miss Deevy to display her supreme talent for depicting subtle character reaction. I recall, on the occasion of the first production of *Katie Roche* at the Abbey, one critic speaking of 'the faultless precision with which Miss Deevy almost minces her way through the human emotions.' *Temporal Powers* is the first play which displays in its fullness this inspired mincing.

Min Donovan, a peasant woman of thirty-two, tired of poverty, is, like Ellie Irwin, seeking a man with something in him of the heroic stature. She looks for him in the person of her drudging, unaffectedly pious husband. To a neighbour who remonstrates with her, she replies, 'I'm not asking that he'd outdo the sun, but only his neighbour.' Under the pressure of her urging he retains some stolen money, and is almost jailed as a consequence. Min informs him that she is proud of him, and the play ends rather sorrowfully on their parting, at least temporarily, while he seeks a living in America.

An interval of three years followed, and then *The King of Spain's Daughter* was produced at the Abbey in 1935. It is a return to the one-act form of *In Search of Valour*, but is an altogether more considerable work. A will-o'-the-wisp light of genius plays and flickers over this slender piece. Above all, it plays over Annie Kinsella, the waif, the philanderer, the dreamer of heroic dreams, 'sailin' out into the sun, and to adventure', the breaker of poor Jim Harris's heart. And what is it that finally makes the idea of marrying him bearable? It is her discovery that he has, with dour persistency, week after week for four long years, ever since a certain day when she had taunted him with his poverty, put by two shillings until he now has twenty pounds saved. He has done a rare deed, and become lifted up into a worthy mate for her untamable spirit. 'I think he is a man that — supposin' he was jealous — might cut your throat.'

And so we come to the greatest of Teresa Deevy's achievements, that gentle masterpiece, that simple and peerless work stamped with the authentic stamp of genius — *Katie Roche*. Katie Roche, a young girl living more or less as a servant in the house of the sister of her future husband, Stanislaus Gregg, is the illegitimate child of educated parents, but has had her own education neglected. Stanislaus, a middle-aged architect and a man of considerable talents, is dismayed to find, on his return from Dublin after a long absence, how wild she is. Nevertheless he marries her.

She is proud of her husband, and has ambitions to influence and inspire his work. But he treats her throughout, save for one or two moments of passion, as little more than a child. She attempts to force his respect by arousing his jealousy. She flirts openly with a local youth who had wished to marry her. The only result of her risky manoeuvre is that her husband leaves her and returns to Dublin.

He seldom visits the house thereafter. In his absence, and during his rare appearances, Katie tries to be a good wife to him. He arrives one day to find her, in circumstances mainly innocent, concealing the same youth in the room. The play ends with his taking her, a country girl who had known but one scene and but one life, away with him. Thus the play ends upon the sorrowful note that do most of Teresa Deevy's, but it is a sorrow lighted up with hope, because it is faced by Katie with her characteristic dash and high courage. 'I was looking for something great to do — sure now I have it.' Thus she shows herself a true scion of a noble line of heroines 'looking for something great to do'.

In *Katie Roche* this idea, stated baldly and humorously in *In Search of Valour*, more deeply and maturely in *Temporal Powers*, is given the supreme, most subtle expression. It is not isolated nor underlined, for it is fused with all that Irish matter-of-factness, those flashes of devilment followed by meekness, that deep religious sense breaking suddenly into incongruous practical considerations whose incongruity is only half unconscious, because a lively sensitiveness to the humour of a situation is the Irish temperament. Katie Roche, wayward, spirited, wilful, meek, restless, fascinating, maddening and endearing, childlike, courageous, tragic — there is no one quite like her in dramatic literature.

Another full-length play, *The Wild Goose*, was produced at the Abbey in 1936. It is a fine play, but not quite of the quality of *Katie Roche* and *Temporal Powers*. Perhaps we miss those wonderful heroines of Teresa Deevy, for in *The Wild Goose*, set in the seventeenth century Ireland of hunted priests and cottages burned over the heads of those that sheltered them, it is Martin Shea who holds the stage, and it is a meek and sad Eileen Connolly who weds him, and loses him to the Irish Brigade fighting Ireland's battles in France.

Miss Deevy's plays — at the time this article was written — have been broadcast from Sweden, Australia and London, but never from her native land. *The King of Spain's Daughter* has appeared in the *Theatre Arts Monthly* and the *Dublin Magazine*. *Katie Roche* was included by Messrs Victor Gollancz in their *Famous Plays 1935–1936*, and is scheduled for a production in the West End. *Katie Roche*, *The King of Spain's Daughter* and *The Wild Goose* have been published together in one volume by Messrs Macmillan and Co.

Brigid and the Mountain
Sean Dorman

On my right was the mighty and bare peak of Mount Shanhoun, in shape and proportion an almost perfect pyramid. Brigid stood by the door watching me. She wore a plaid kerchief over her head and tied under her chin.

Agnes's buxom body might have become more buxom, as her mother Brigid alleged, yet secretly I was attracted by it. She was so compact, so rounded, so sturdy and vigorous, so shapely, yes, even graceful, as she moved rhythmically, as I had seen her one day weeding a field of potatoes.

Under its first title of 'Valley of Graneen', before a revision, *Brigid and the Mountain* was Recommended by the Book Society. *The Times Literary Supplement*, after a long review, summed up the book in the phrase, 'beautiful restraint'. *The Scotsman* wrote, 'His sketches are vivid and sincere. The physical aspects of the valley are described with remarkable clarity, and Mr Dorman is equally successful in his portraits of the inhabitants.' *The Sydney Morning Herald* wrote, in the course of a review of over two hundred words, 'These sketches of Donegal are delightful.' *Irish Independent*: 'Of his days in the valley, his friendships, and his talks, (Sean Dorman) has moulded a book of much charm. There is writing of grace and high degree . . . Withal, it is a notable book.' *Irish Press*: 'Sean Dorman brought with him a receptive mind, an artists's observant eye, and some writing materials. The result is . . . a very pleasant book.'

ISBN 0 9518119 8 3   Price £4.99

The Raffeen Press

Portrait of My Youth
Sean Dorman

Portrait of My Youth traces the earlier years of a remarkable Irish writer, Sean Dorman. The narrative, always lively, often extremely funny, sweeps the reader along on a bubbling current. There are fascinating glimpses of the British Raj in India as seen through a young child's eyes; of Algiers and Aden as seen through those of an older schoolboy; of student escapades at Oxford and in Paris in a more carefree era; of a visit to an extraordinary French family near Nice and Cannes'; of sexual shenanigans in London's bohemian Chelsea; of difficulties with an alcoholic uncle famous as an Irish playwright; of meetings with literary and theatrical notables: E. M. Forster, Granville Barker, Sean O'Casey, John Betjeman, T. S. Eliot, Barry Fitzgerald, Dame Sybil Thorndike, W. B. Yeats, Laurence Olivier, Deborah Kerr.

'Delightful, humorous, full of marvellous observation.'
Colin Wilson

At the age of fourteen, in his first term at his public school, Sean Dorman was awarded a prize as the best prose writer in the school. He was the winner of an essay competition open to the public schools of Great Britain and Ireland. After graduating at Oxford, he worked as a freelance journalist in London, contributing articles to some twenty periodicals, and ghosting six non-fiction books for a publisher. For five and a half years he edited a theatrical and art magazine in Dublin, and for twenty-six years in England a magazine for writers. His three-volume hardback, *The Selected Works of Sean Dorman*, comprises autobiography, essays, novels, short stories and verse.

ISBN 0 9518119 9 1   Price £4.99

The Raffeen Press

Red Roses for Jenny
Sean Dorman

Red Roses for Jenny . . . What did they mean to her? A father's affection? Or a lover's desire? If they meant either to her, or both to her, then why did she throw them away? Did her mother come to hear of them? Or the wife of the man who gave them to her? And Jim, what did he think? He must have seen them, and surely he must have been disturbed. Was Jenny carrying a child, or was she not? If she were, could Jim succeed on containing the scandal and so protect his mother's feelings? Canon Moss, for all his funny ways, was wise. Was his wisdom sufficient to save them all? And, at the end of the long day, why did Jenny restore the red roses to her office desk again?

After the great success of Sean Dorman's autobiographical first novel, *Brigid and the Mountain*, initially, until revised, entitled 'Valley of Graneen' and, under that title, a Book Society Recommendation; also praised by *The Times Literary Supplement*, *The Irish Press*, *The Scotsman*, Australia's *Sydney Morning Herald*, *Irish Independent*, and many others; Mr Dorman took time off to acquire the technique of the non-autobiographical novel. The result is *Red Roses for Jenny*, with its vivid characters and driving speed of narrative. If the mountain scapes of *Brigid and the Mountain* are fine, no less fine are the seascapes of *Red Roses for Jenny*, with storm scenes as background to a love between a man and a woman no less stormy.

ISBN 0 9518119 7 5 　　　　　　　　　　　　　　　Price £4.99

The Raffeen Press

The Madonna
Sean Dorman

'A great twentieth-century novel.'

Judy Summers, arrested by the sound of men's voices, paused on her way to visit The Madonna. Her cheap gay cotton dress fluttered about her shapely legs. Judy Summers liked men. She liked them very much. Also, it had become imperative that she should acquire a husband . . .

They were beside the little wayside shrine. George saw that Judy's eyes were fixed on the painted Mother cradling in her arms her painted Baby. 'The birth and the feeding have been a great strain on you, darling. Don't you think that Mark ought to go on to the bottle?' Judy was shaking her head vigorously. 'I'd give my life for Mark. I feel — I feel there's something in me of The Madonna.'

George went to Rose. She drew away in hurt pride. He broke down her resistance and swept her into his arms. 'Of course you didn't mean any harm, sweetheart. I've had a very upsetting letter from Judy. I love my wife. She's the mother of my son, but it's been a great strain. You've helped me keep my sanity.' He began to rain down kisses on her brow, her cheeks, her lips. Eyes closed, she held up her face to receive them.

'*The Madonna* reads as inevitably as does Tolstoy and bears out Eliot's, "In my end is my beginning." If it reaches its proper audience, it will be read with a mixture of discovery and relief. The novel is still alive!'
George Sully

ISBN 0 9518119 6 7   Price £4.99

The Raffeen Press

Physicians, Priests & Physicists
Sean Dorman

The most potent reason for Sean Dorman's writing this book arose from the existence of his magazine *Commentary*. This monthly appeared in Dublin in the forties during five and a half years. At an average of two thousand copies a month, he felt it to be a certainty that copies still lurked in collections both public and private, even possibly in newspapers files, there to haunt him. In his youthful pugnacity, had he somtimes overstated his case and fallen into folly? If so, the only way out was to republish his essays or editorials, with inserted toning down remarks where such seemed needed.

The essays cover the subjects of: literary censorship; cancer, heart disease and arthritis-resisting diets and exercises, including exercises underwater in a hot bath (his wife suffered from arthritis of the hip, and died of smoking and alcohol-induced cancer); the existence or non-existence of God as found in the Bible; or in the discoveries about the universe as found in the work of scientists such as Aristotle, Ptolemy, Copernicus, Galileo, Kepler, Newton, Einstein (his Special Theory, and his General Theory, of Relativity, are explained in simple terms), and the somewhat later quantum mechanics, and the twistor and superstring theories. Also particle physics. Other essays are entitled: 'How to Rear a Baby', 'The Adventure of Marriage ', Jews and Gentiles'.

ISBN 1 9012430 0 1   Price £3.99

The Raffeen Press

The Strong Man
Sean Dorman

The Strong Man, a comedy in three acts, can lay no claims either to distinction or to having been performed on a stage. But it can claim to have been read by a considerable number of people who have reported that it caused them not only to smile but, on occasion, to laugh outright. Should something that has given rise to smiles, and even laughter, be left upon a shelf, or be entombed in a drawer? Of course not. It should be produced in a book. Also produced in this book are three theatre critiques. In days gone by, Ireland gave to literature great playwrights from that seeming hotbed of dramatic genius, Dublin University: William Congreve, George Farquhar, Oliver Goldsmith. Since then there have been: John Millington Synge, Samuel Beckett (both from the same university), William Butler Yeats, Oscar Wilde, Bernard Shaw, Sean O'Casey. Well known, but perhaps less well known than they ought to be, are Denis Johnston and Teresa Deevy. I have devoted a critique to each of them. Also to William Shakespeare, an Englishman, I'm told. The trouble with William Shakespeare, is that he has been allowed, unfortunately, to develop into a cult figure. Not only are his great plays produced, but his lesser pieces also are reverently laid out upon the stage, thus almost certainly denying many hours of theatre time to others with better work to offer. Such a lesser piece, here reviewed, is *Twelve Night*.

ISBN 1 901243 05 2   Price £3.99

The Raffeen Press

Sex and the Reverend Strong
Sean Dorman

When the Bishop, at his Palace, was looking straight at you, you knew where you were with him. But when his gaze wandered out through the window of his study to settle on the Cathedral, you no longer were so sure. 'With ever more people in England turning to crime, the Church of England is in danger of getting out of touch. The clergy, to an increasing degree, should be drawn from the criminal classes. No priest, without at least one previous conviction, should be considered for a bishopric. The Archbishop of Canterbury should be an old lag.'

A girl was approaching the Archdeacon. Her pretty eyes looked with favour on his great height, the broad-brimmed shovel hat ashine in the sunlight, his heavy eyebrows, his full mouth and powerful chin, the fine black cloth of the cassock covering his broad chest, his frock-coat; his black breeches, stockings, gaiters, showing a well-turned leg. Yes, there was power there — and money. 'Hello, big boy! Like me to show you a good time?' She put a small soft hand on his sleeve. He drew himself up. 'As a jewel of gold in a swine's snout, so is a fair woman which is without discretion. Proverbs, chapter eleven, verse twenty-two.' 'I've plenty of discretion, big boy. You visit me any time, and no one will ever know.'

As Robin, Vicar of Ferne, reached home, it was to find his wife Mary pretending indignation. 'So my lunch cooking isn't good enough! It's got to be lunch at the *Palace* now!' Robin, in imitation of the Archdeacon, folded his hands behind his back and began to pace the drawing-room with ponderous steps. Finally, pausing by the piano, he announced to it, 'A continual dropping in a very rainy day and a contentious woman are alike. Proverbs, chapter twenty-seven, verse fifteen.' Mary, her hands folded behind her back, trundled clumsily towards the bookcase. 'A man who cannot get home for lunch, is like a buffalo which cannot find a water-hole. Proverbs, chapter five thousand, verse one million.' The Vicar of

Ferne turned on her, his face apparently contorted with wrath. She shrieked, fled the drawing-room, and up the stairs. The Reverend Robin Strong rushed after her, bellowing, it seemed, in ungovernable rage. She ran into the bedroom, he hot on her heels. The sound of further shrieks emerged, followed by a struggle . . . There, we close the door.

ISBN 1 901243 10 9   Price £4.99

The Raffeen Press